Samual L. Parrish

Historical, biographical, and descriptive catalogue of the objects exhibited at the Southampton Art Museum

Samual L. Parrish

Historical, biographical, and descriptive catalogue of the objects exhibited at the Southampton Art Museum

ISBN/EAN: 9783742862631

Manufactured in Europe, USA, Canada, Australia, Japa

Cover: Foto ©Andreas Hilbeck / pixelio.de

Manufactured and distributed by brebook publishing software (www.brebook.com)

Samual L. Parrish

Historical, biographical, and descriptive catalogue of the objects exhibited at the Southampton Art Museum

MAIN ENTRANCE TO THE GARDEN AND MUSEUM.

HISTORICAL,

BIOGRAPHICAL, AND DESCRIPTIVE

CATALOGUE

OF

THE OBJECTS EXHIBITED AT THE
SOUTHAMPTON ART MUSEUM,

ESTABLISHED AT

Southampton, New York,

BY

SAMUEL L. PARRISH,

In the Year 1897.

NEW YORK:
BENJAMIN H. TYRREL.
1898.

To

HENRY G. MARQUAND, ESQ.,

PRESIDENT OF THE

METROPOLITAN MUSEUM OF ART

OF NEW YORK,

To whose Liberality and Devotion that most Complete

Museum in America is so Greatly Indebted

for its Success, this Catalogue

is, with Permission,

INSCRIBED.

TABLE OF CONTENTS.

PERSONAGES REPRESENTED IN THE TAPESTRY:

Edward the Confessor, King of England.

Harold, Earl, and later, for about ten months, King of England.

William the Conqueror, Duke of Normandy, and later King of England.

Odo, Bishop of Bayeux, Half Brother of William the Conqueror.

Guy, Count of Ponthieu.

Conan, Count of Brittany.

Robert, Count of Mortain.

Turold, a Dwarf.

Aelfgyva.

Ealdgyth, wife of Harold.

Stigand, Archbishop of Canterbury.

Wadard.

Vital, a Norman Scout.

Leofwine, Brother of King Harold.
Gyrth, Brother of King Harold.
Eustace, Count of Boulogne.
Norman and Saxon Knights, Soldiers, Sailors, Peasants,
    etc.

SOUTH SIDE OF THE MUSEUM BUILDING.
The Catalpa Tree.

HISTORICAL, BIOGRAPHICAL, AND DESCRIPTIVE CATALOGUE.

PREFACE.

The object in establishing this small Museum has **been** to give to the people of Southampton, and the surrounding country, and especially to the younger generation, an opportunity to enjoy the influences generally recognized as incident to such an institution. It is the desire and intention, so far as circumstances will **permit,** to make it auxiliary, on its educational side, to **the Public** School and Library. In most European countries, the desirability of this form of education is so strongly felt that the government itself, or the municipality, generally takes the initiative, at least in the larger centres of population. Owing to the concentration of population in the older countries, and the

greater interest there manifested in institutions of this
kind, the distance of the bulk of the people from some
point of educational and artistic interest is usually comparatively small. The result is that, in the course of
the year, large numbers will have often availed themselves of the opportunity offered to visit the museum or
gallery of the neighboring town. This fact will be
readily appreciated by any one who has had occasion
to watch the crowds that throng the English and Continental galleries on some holiday that brings together
the people from the outlying districts. In this connection it will be noted that there is already a tendency
in our own country to follow the example of the older
civilization of Europe. This tendency has recently
taken form by introducing, into the public schools of
New York, photographs and pictures that will excite
an interest in the study of the great works of architecture and art that abound in foreign lands. Naturally,
under the conditions surrounding this undertaking,
there can be nothing in the nature of an attempt to repro-
duce the result accomplished by even the most modest of
the American and European institutions, inaugurated
and sustained as they are by such powerful influences
continually at work for their enlargement and improve-
ment. Especially is this limitation experienced in the
domain of painting and original works of statuary. In
regard to plaster copies, however, of which many
of the museums so largely avail themselves, the
situation is entirely different. Here we are on com-

paratively common ground, for the art of reproduction
has been brought to such a point of perfection, that
excellent plaster copies can be had of nearly all the
great works of antiquity that have come down to us,
as well as copies of the creations of later date, rivalling
in many cases even those of the classic period itself.
Thus, copies of the works of Phidias and Praxitiles and
Michael Angelo and Donatello, and others of the great
sculptors whose works have been, and will always continue to be, the admiration of successive generations,
are readily obtainable. It will, of course, be understood that to the mind, and practised eye and hand, of
the sculptor, no reproduction can ever take the place
of the original work. On the other hand it is believed
that to those who find pleasure in the contemplation of
the beautiful in form, a skilful reproduction will very
strongly appeal, and have a valuable educational influence. This fact has been greatly appreciated in our
own country by the men who are at the head of the
museums in our principal cities. The result is that in
New York, Boston, Chicago, Philadelphia and Washington, and numerous other smaller places, the real
treasures, speaking broadly from the point of view of
artistic education, housed by the elaborate and
costly structures that have arisen as the result
of a desire to cultivate the fine arts, are not so
much the modern pictures, interesting and valuable as
many of them are, as the plaster reproductions of the
antique and Renaissance sculpture, those masterpieces

of the genius **of man** at its highest **period** of development in the **world of** art.

This, then, **is** the motive of an **attempt** to create this
small museum, an attempt **which** could only **end in**
failure were it not for the possibilities afforded by **the
art of** reproduction. Nor is this art exhausted when
only forms of ideal beauty have been offered for exhibition. Still another, **and in** some aspects **more** important element of value, **is** the opportunity afforded to
awaken and stimulate **an** interest in the **study of** history.
In a community **like** ours, based **upon the** general
intelligence **of the** people, and fostered **by** the common-
school **system, the** experience **of other** countries, so
necessary **to a** right understanding **of our** own, can only
be learned **by** the study of history. On this point the
following words of Carlyle will **be** recognized as **spoken
with authority:**

"In **all my** poor historical investigations it has been,
and always will be, one of the most primary wants to
procure a bodily likeness **of the** personage inquired
after, a good portrait, **if** such exists; failing that, even
an indifferent, if sincere one.

"In short, any representation made **by** a faithful
human creature of that face and figure which he saw
with **his** eyes, and which I can never see with mine, is
now valuable to me and much better than none at all.
It has always struck me that historical portrait galleries
far transcend in worth **all** other kinds of national
collections of pictures whatever; that, in fact, they

LOOKING NORTH TOWARD THE ORGAN, WITH THE ROMAN IMPERIAL BUSTS ON EACH
SIDE OF THE HALL.

ought to exist **in** every **country** as among the most popular and cherished national possessions. Lord Chancellor Clarendon made a brave attempt in that kind **for** England, but his house and gallery fell asunder in **a** sad way."

What is **true of** portraits is also true of portrait busts. In **the** case of the latter there is also the added practical consideration that, owing to the greater dura**bility** of the material, we have now, and successive gen**erations** will continue to have, an opportunity to study **the** features of many of the great men of antiquity, as **well** as those of more recent times, which would have been forever lost, had we been compelled **to rely upon** the art of portrait painting alone. In **a small museum** like this there can naturally be exhibited **but a very** limited number of the hundreds of more **or less** authentic and interesting portrait busts that have come down to us through the ages, beginning **as** they do in the very twilight of history.

In the selection of the marble and plaster reproductions here exhibited, no especial order or plan has been observed, the intention being to have the hall contain gen**erally such** objects as have a world-wide reputation, **either from** their artistic merit **or** historical associa**tion.** Accompanying each object exhibited is a biographical or historical statement, longer or shorter as the case may be, giving in outline the history of the individual, if a bust, or of the work of art, if an ideal creation, with the name of the sculptor, when known,

and in the case of copies of the antique, a statement of
when and where the originals were found, and their
present location. From time to time explanatory and
historical foot notes have been added, which, it was
thought, might prove of interest, and in some cases, for
the same reason, the text itself has been enlarged beyond the scope of a descriptive, or even strictly historical, catalogue as related to what is contained in the
hall itself.

Of the historical reproductions, it is believed that the
collection of the half length effigies of some of the
Plantagenet and Tudor kings and queens will be found
particularly interesting, especially to the students of
English history. The original effigies, in full length,
either in bronze, brass, or alabaster, being works of the
period, lie recumbent upon the tombs of the persons
represented, mostly in Westminster Abbey or in Canterbury Cathedral. The half length effigies here exhibited
are taken from electrotype reproductions now to be
seen in the National Portrait Gallery, an institution
established in London about two years ago, under the
auspices of the British Government. This institution
has carried out on a grand scale the opinion and
sentiment of Carlyle, as embodied in the quotation
given above.

The collection of pictures, shown here at Southampton,
has been made, for the most part, during several visits
to Italy in the past few years. The pictures were
obtained principally in Venice and Florence, and their

respective neighborhoods, though some of them were acquired in other continental cities, and a few in London and New York. In most cases the name of the artist is unknown, though the pictures themselves belong to recognized schools or periods of Italian art, ranging from about the beginning of the **15th** to the latter part of **the** 17th centuries, and are generally painted **on panel.** During that period Italy **was a vast artistic** workshop, and following **the sentiment of the** period, the subjects chosen for representation **were** usually of a religious character, or portraits, interspersed with large decorative pictures representing festive occasions, generally with a bible story as the subject, or allegorical scenes taken from the classic poets. Landscape, except as an accessory, and scenes from common life, were seldom taken, in Italy at least, for the purpose of artistic illustration, during the period of Italian supremacy in art.

Some of the pictures here shown are therefore, doubtless, from the hands of pupils of some of the great Italian masters—pupils whose name and fame were perhaps only local during their own time, but whose works nevertheless contain something of the spirit of the period represented by the Italian Renaissance. In cases where direct attributions have been made to some of the minor painters, the pictures are submitted to the judgment of those who have made a study of this epoch of artistic development.

In regard to the reproductions in plaster and marble,

we are on more certain ground, for these have been taken from the authenticated original works which are scattered, for the most part, through the churches and museums of Europe. The actual reproductions here shown were acquired in Florence, Paris, London and New York. The "Laocoön," "The Faun of Praxitiles," "The Wrestlers," "The Winged Victory of Samathrace," and some others, were obtained from the "Atelier de Moulage," as it is called, or plaster cast establishment, attached to the Museum of the Louvre in Paris, and conducted by the government. The plaster reproduction of the Parthenon Frieze was obtained from the Metropolitan Museum of Art of New York.

The autotype copy of the Bayeux Tapestry was acquired in London, and taken from plates in the possession of the British Government, Science and Art Department.

It will be noted that the collection is confined almost exclusively to such objects as illustrate or represent the history, biography, and art of Greece, Italy and England; the three countries, above all others, to which we in America, directly or indirectly, owe all that is most valuable in our intellectual and political life.

In the reading-room, to the west of the main hall, will be found, among the books relating to travel and the history of art, certain volumes which will enable the visitor so desiring to acquire more accurate and extended information in regard to the biography of the individuals represented by the statuary and casts, and

THE LILY POND AND ARBORETUM.

of the history **of the other objects contained in this col-**
lection.

Surrounding the building itself is about **an** acre of
ground, containing the nucleus of a small botanical
garden. In the reading-room will be found a certain
number of books on botany.

SAMUEL L. PARRISH.

New York.
March, 1898.

Since the preceding Preface was written, a swift and
uncontrollable current of events has swept the world
away from its old moorings, and brought our country
face to face with difficulties, dangers, and problems little
dreamed of but a few short months ago. Whatever may
be the outcome of the present Spanish-American war,
however, there is at least one fact that, in its far-reaching
import, stands forth clearly above all others; and that
is the inherent similarity of aim and purpose existing
between England and **America** in **their** relations toward
the rest of the world.

With their old and narrow bickerings and jealousies
now happily relegated to the background, let us hope
forever, so far as any serious or threatening developments may be concerned, there should be an ever-widen-

ing interest **in** the sympathetic study, **by** each, of the history and political evolution of the other. Looked at from this point of view the burden of **inquiry** naturally falls more particularly upon us, for from the **time** of the Norman Conquest to the beginnings of the **settlement** of our own country, a period of nearly six hundred years, the history of England is equally the history of all of us who are of English descent, and collaterally the history also of all our fellow countrymen, who enjoy the privileges of a government founded in essentials upon the successful struggles for personal, political and civil liberty, waged through the centuries on English soil. **The** national character developed by **those** struggles **is part** and parcel **of our** inheritance, **and the** capacity **to** assimilate foreign elements shown **by us,** becomes but an additional tribute **to** the **solidity, strength,** and world-wide influence of **the** principles **derived** from our English ancestry, principles accepted in good faith by none more than by those of other racial antecedents, who, by incorporation into our body politic, have become too, the political descendants of the race from which we spring.

In considering this subject further, it is well to remember that the Americans of 1776 were also but the political (and in many cases lineal), descendants of the Englishmen who stood for liberty in 1640 and 1688, and that nowhere is this fact more cheerfully acknowledged than in England itself. In the National Portrait Gallery in London, England's Walhalla, the portrait

of George Washington **hangs on** the line with the
great Englishmen of his **time.** Of the insignifi-
cant minority of Englishmen to-day who honestly
dislike, or even hate, America and its institutions it would doubtless be found that in nine
cases out of ten, they are drawn from the ranks of the
political or actual descendants of the men who in
former centuries were willing to sacrifice the liberty
and well-being of their country to the prerogative and
claim of divine right of the King; men whose theories of
government, had they prevailed, would have landed England where Spain now finds herself, namely, in the
rear rather than in the vanguard of modern progress
and civilization.

And yet another consideration. There are doubtless in America to-day hundreds of thousands of
men in whose veins, unknown to themselves, flows at
least some particle of the blood of the sturdy
English, Irish, and Welsh soldiers whose discipline, courage, and constancy in the hour of danger
turned impending defeat into victory, against vast
numerical odds, on the fields of Crécy, Poitiers and
Agincourt. Add to these the American descendants
of the Englishmen who fought on a dozen fields in
England itself to uphold their liberties against the en-
croachments of arbitrary power, and the numbers may
well be swelled into the millions. Thus can we
realize that in our common inheritance of noble tradi-

tions the talk of "blood being thicker than water," is no idle figure of rhetoric.

These then being historical facts, it is beyond the scope of this short note to consider what modifications, for better or for worse, our strong national individuality may have grafted upon the parent system.

In any event it is confidently submitted that the developments of the past few months cannot but add interest to the study of such objects in this collection as tend to illustrate the history of England.

S. L. P.

Southampton, N. Y., June, 1898.

PREFACE TO THE ILLUSTRATED EDITION.

Since the Museum was established and this Catalogue written, in 1898, both the grounds and building have been enlarged, the latter in 1902, through the generous interest of my brother Mr. James C. Parrish. Into the new fire proof hall presented by him have been moved most of the original pictures described in the Catalogue. The museum building is now in the shape of a cross, and stands about one hundred and fifty feet back from the street. It is built partly of brick and partly of wood, with a maximum length and width of one hundred and thirty-five and one hundred and two feet respectively. It is situated in a park of about three acres in extent at a central point in the village, its adjoining neighbors being the Public Library and the Municipal Building.

During a visit to Italy and France in the spring of 1900 I became much impressed with the antique busts of the Roman Emperors, to be found for the

most part in the galleries of the Vatican and the
Capitol at Rome, in the Uffizi at Florence, and in
the so-called "Hall of Augustus" in the Museum of
the Louvre at Paris. With the invaluable aid of the
late Mr. Augustus St. Gaudens, whose acquaintance
I had the good fortune to renew in Paris in the sum-
mer of 1900 at the time of the Paris Exposition, I
made a selection, by means of photographs, from the
many differing busts, of the first eighteen of the
Caesars, beginning with Julius and ending with Commodus, and, in Florence, had them reproduced, in
marble, of uniform semi-heroic size, with classic
shoulders added where the head alone had survived
the destructive hand of time. These busts of decorative, but more especially of historical and archaeological value, now adorn the new hall at South-
hampton. In addition to the Roman imperial busts
other objects of artistic interest have been added to
the collection from time to time during the past ten
or twelve years, consisting for the most part of reproductions in marble and terra cotta of Greek, Roman,
and Renaissance sculpture, but as a description of
these would have required a rearrangement of the
Catalogue it was thought best to confine the illustra-
tions to those objects which formed a part of the collection at the time it was written. At a later date, however, it is my intention to issue an addendum to the
present edition in the form of a separate volume which
shall contain half tone reproductions of the eighteen

imperial busts, now to be seen at Southampton, together with short monographs upon the lives and characters of the emperors represented, after the manner of those in this volume relating to Augustus and Tiberius Ceasar.

SAMUEL L. PARRISH.

Southampton, Long Island,
    August, 1912.

LOOKING TOWARD THE SOUTH ALCOVE.

BAYEUX TAPESTRY.

NOTE.

The Bayeux Tapestry, of the exact size of the original, has been reproduced by the autotype process, and being colored by hand, the reproduction here shown at Southampton presents a striking resemblance to the original work. The plates are in the possession of the British Government, but with that liberality which characterizes the English in all matters pertaining to the acquisition and diffusion of knowledge, are loaned from time to time for the purpose of making copies.

One of these reproductions is to be seen in London in the South Kensington Museum, and, besides the one exhibited here, there is another in the

Pennsylvania **Museum, in Fairmount Park, Phila**-
delphia.

For those desiring to make **a more accurate**
study in detail of the various **scenes, a running**
commentary, compiled from **various sources has**
been prepared, and follows **the general summary**
here given. Especial recognition **in this work is**
hereby accorded to the very valuable catalogue **which**
has been prepared under the supervision of **the au**-
thorities of the Pennsylvania Museum, compiled from
Mr. Fowke's work on the Tapestry, and that of
l'abbé **J**. Laffetay.

EAST SIDE OF THE MUSEUM.

BAYEUX TAPESTRY.

The so-called Bayeux Tapestry is in fact a piece **of** embroidery on a linen band 20 inches wide, and 230 feet long. It is a pictorial history.

The original embroidery, framed and covered **with** glass, is now in a small museum, to which it **was** removed from the Cathedral, in the little Norman town **of** Bayeux. **It** is an authentic work of the latter part **of** the **eleventh** century or the beginning of the twelfth, though its actual authorship is a matter of conjecture only. Some authorities attribute it directly to Matilda, the wife of William the Conqueror, assisted by the ladies of her court. Others assign it to English workmen, acting under the direction of the Empress Matilda, granddaughter of the Conqueror. The best authorities, however, attribute it, largely on the basis of certain internal evidence, to Norman workmanship under the

direction of Odo, Bishop of Bayeux, half-brother of
William, and believe it was made for the decoration of
the Cathedral of Bayeux, which was rebuilt by Odo in
1077. The last theory is the one maintained by Free-
man in his "History of the Norman Conquest." In
any event, however, the tapestry is generally believed
to be a practically contemporary work with the events
it so rudely and yet so graphically describes. It remained in the Cathedral of Bayeux for about four
hundred years before exciting sufficient attention to be
mentioned, at least so far as any existing record is concerned, as the earliest reference to it now known is to
be found in an inventory of the effects of the cathedral
taken in 1476. In the next two hundred and fifty
years nothing is heard of it outside of the cathedral,
where it was used for decorative purposes on certain
feast days. It was then hung round the nave, and
being exactly sufficient to go around the walls, the
basis on which its length was originally determined is
thus indicated. In 1724 it came under the notice of
the French Academy of Inscriptions, when its extraordinary historical value was at once recognized, and
from that time to the present day has excited the greatest interest as being for practical purposes the most
valuable document that has come down to us of a period
so unfortunately lacking in authentic historical records.
It is divided into seventy-two scenes, each scene being
separated from its neighbor by trees or a building, embroidered simply for the purpose of marking the divid-

ing line. The original is done with a needle in eight
different colors of worsted, and gives a history of the
Norman Conquest of England from a Norman point of
view, taking care to emphasize the points making for
the justice of William's claim to the English throne.
By the crude employment of the different colors an
attempt is made to create some sort of perspective,
otherwise lacking. It will be noted, for instance, that
a green horse will have his off legs painted red, while
those of a yellow horse will be blue. In addition to its
interest as a pictorial narrative of events, it has an
especial value as furnishing us, in however rude a form,
with a fairly accurate idea of some of the costumes, as
well as the architecture and arms, of the time of the
Conquest, including points of especial interest to a
seafaring people in those scenes which represent the
embarking of Harold and the boat building of William.
In these respects it closely resembles some of the most
ancient Egyptian mural decorations, particularly those
to be seen in the rock tomb of Beni-Hasan on the Nile.
One of the features of the tapestry is the embroidery
of a superscription, in Latin, above each scene, giving
a short, simple and at times almost quaint description
of the scene represented underneath. A short outline
of the pictorial story is as follows:

In the first panel Harold, son of the earl Godwine,
and brother-in-law to the English king, Edward the
Confessor, appears before the king in his royal palace
at Westminster, and is evidently being sent by the

king on a mission to William of Normandy, presumably to inform the latter that, upon the death of Edward,
William shall succeed to the throne of England.
Harold then starts off gaily with his retinue, and on
their way to the south coast of England to embark for
Normandy, a spirited hawking scene with hounds is
shown on the embroidery. Arrived at his manor of Bosham, Harold goes to church to obtain a blessing on his
journey, but quickly returns to the manor house for a
carouse, before setting sail. He and his companions are
seen pledging each other in bowls and horns of wine. The
next scene is one of the most interesting of all, showing
Harold and his companions in the act of embarking.
These panels should be studied carefully, as giving a
most interesting exhibition of the construction of the
ships of the period. Being driven by a stress of weather
on the coast of France, the English party are taken
prisoners, in accordance with the inhospitable custom
of the time, by the lord of that part of the country, a
certain count Guy, of Ponthieu. Several panels are
devoted to this portion of their experiences. William,
however, hearing of Harold's unfortunate position,
sends messengers to the count and commands that the
prisoners be set free and conducted to him at his
capital of Rouen. They arrive at Rouen, and, after
some interesting scenes at the Norman court, accom-
pany William on an expedition against the count of
Brittany. During this expedition, Harold has occasion
to show his great strength, for which he was famous,

by rescuing some soldiers from certain well-known
quicksands which the company were obliged to cross.
The following scenes represent the defeat of Conan,
count of Brittany, by William's troops, and Harold,
for his bravery, is knighted by the Duke. They then
return to Bayeux, when Harold takes his celebrated
oath. The tradition is that Harold swore to marry
William's daughter, and to give his own sister in
marriage to the Norman Duke, and uphold the claim
of William to the English throne upon the death of
Edward. On the embroidery is shown the chest which
William caused to be filled with the holiest relics and
then covered with a pall. Harold has his hand upon
the chest as he takes the oath. The ceremony finished,
the chest is uncovered, and the relics then shown for
the first time to Harold. The next scene represents the
return of the Saxon earl, Harold, as he embarks for
England in a ship manned by Norman sailors, the
difference between Saxon and Norman almost throughout the tapestry being denoted by certain distinguish-
ing marks, particularly the arrangement of the beard,
the Saxon wearing a moustache, while the Norman is
clean shaven. Upon his arrival in England, Harold
rides post-haste to Westminster to report to the king,
and is received by Edward, represented as enfeebled
by age and nearing his end. The king is seated upon
his throne with his sceptre reversed in his hand.
Harold, conveniently forgetting his oath, in the presence
of certain friends, whom he has assembled around the

deathbed of the king, prompts one of his friends to urge Edward to name him, Harold, as his successor. The king replies that he has already named Duke William. Harold himself then personally urges his claim, and the king in his feebleness replies: "Let the English name the Duke or Harold, King, as they please; I consent," and saying this he dies. Upon the day of the Confessor's death Harold is chosen king, and two of the nobles notify him of his election, and bring him the crown and official axe, and he is crowned as repre-sented in the scene. Then follows the incident of the comet, this illustration being the earliest known pictorial representation of this celestial object, and supposed to be ominous of the coming invasion of England. The news of Harold's coronation was forth-with carried to Normandy, and William, with his accustomed decision of character, at once sets about to build ships for the descent upon Eng-land. The men bring stores and provisions for the ships, which are being hauled down to the sea, and the duke embarks in the historical ship "Mora," given him by his wife, and the next morning, being the 28th of September, 1066, lands in England, at Pevensey, unop-posed. Then follows the disembarkation of the horses and men, who start out to forage for breakfast, and we see the lasso being used for this purpose. The country people fleeing from their homes at the approach of the Normans, the foragers find it an easy task to collect material for breakfast, and the following scenes tell an interesting story of the preparation and enjoyment of the morning meal. Bishop Odo, William's half-brother, a very notable person in those times, is seen seated on the duke's left hand, and asks a blessing. Then follows a council of war between William and his two half-brothers, the Bishop and count Robert of Mortain. As a result of the council, orders are given to build a fort at Hastings, and we see the orders being carried out. After some intermediate scenes the great battle of Hastings is begun, and at one time Harold is shown alone wielding his two-handed battle-axe against fearful odds. Bishop Odo is also seen clad in armor, seeking to rally some of the Norman troops who had been seized with panic. The report having gone abroad that William had been killed, and the Normans wavering, the duke rushed into the midst of the fight, and, raising his helmet, exclaims, "I am here!" or perhaps makes use of the very words embroidered on the scene, "Hic Est Wilel Dux!" When the Normans at this time were hardest pressed, William gave his celebrated order, "Shoot *upwards*, Norman archers!" Of the falling arrows one pierced the eye of Harold, while valiantly wielding his axe in the thick of the fight. As he sought to pluck the arrow from his eye, the shaft broke, and he fell mortally wounded. The English, demoralized by the loss of their king, flee, as represented in the scene. The battle is over and the story of the tapestry is told.

DETAILED COMMENTARY ON THE SEPARATE SCENES OF THE BAYEUX TAPESTRY.

SCREENING A BROKAGE
ANIS: WHERE HAROLD, DUKE OF THE ENGLISH, AND HIS KNIGHTS RIDE TO BOSHAM
AND THE CHURCH

Figure 17-26

EDWARD REX.

King Eadward.

The opening scene represents King Eadward the Confessor, seated upon his throne, in an apartment of the palace at Westminster, upon the site where now stands Westminster Hall. Attention is called to the checkered work on the face of the tower. Examples of this kind of work are still to be seen in Normandy. It will be noticed also that Eadward's crown, as well as the sceptre, is ornamented with *fleurs-de-lys*. Of the two persons to whom his remarks are addressed the taller is Harold, son of the earl Godwine, and brother-in-law to the king (Eadward having married Editha, Harold's sister). The more usual interpretation given to this scene is that it represents Eadward giving instruc-

tions to Harold to proceed on a mission to Normandy
to inform Duke William that he has been nominated
by Eadward as his successor to the English throne.

VBI: HAROLD DVX: ANGLORVM: ET SVI
MILITES: EQVITANT: AD BOSHAM:

*Where Harold, Duke of the English, and his knights
ride to Bosham.*

Bosham was a manorial estate inherited by Harold
from his father on the southern coast of England. From
this point he prepares for his voyage across the channel. Hawking was a favorite amusement among the
nobles in England, as well as in France, at the time of
the Conquest, and Harold and his companions indulge
in this pastime on their way to the coast. Harold's
dress is here worthy of remark, for the cloak he wears,
fastened at the right shoulder, with a clasp, is an evidence of his rank, being worn only by people of high
birth. Observe, also, that here, and for the most part
throughout the tapestry, the Saxons wear moustaches,
while the Normans are generally clean shaven. That
the equipments of the horses, saddles, bridles and
stirrups, as shown in this scene, should so nearly correspond to many of those of our own time, is an interesting fact.

ECCLESIA.

The Church.

As soon as Harold arrives at Bosham he at once proceeds to the church to ask a blessing on the enterprise,

HERE HAROLD SET SAIL UPON THE SEA AND WITH SAILS FILLED BY THE WIND
CAME TO THE LAND OF COUNT GUY.

Page 17.

but, **this duty over,** he forthwith returns to the manor
house to **indulge in** a jovial carouse before setting sail.
This interlude takes place in an upper hall reached by
a flight of steps on the outside, and the gay party are
seen pledging each other in bowls and horns of wine.

HIC HAROLD: MARE NAVIGAVIT :· ET
VELIS: VENTO: PLENIS VENIT: IN
TERRA: WIDONIS COMITIS.

*Here Harold set sail upon the sea and with sails filled
by the wind came to the land of Count Guy.*

In this scene we see Harold and his companions
who have not forgotten their hawk and dogs, wading
out to the ship, which is fitted with one mast only, and
square rigged **with** a prominent figurehead. The vessel is also arranged for rowers and is steered by a pad-
dle, in this case handled by Harold, who is evidently
also giving directions in regard to the setting of the
sail. The interlocked shields of the soldiers along the
side of the vessel are doubtless for the purpose of in-
suring a reasonably dry passage across the channel.
Arrived safely on the other side we notice the various
incidents of the landing, men taking in sail, poling the
vessel, and one man in the bow ready to let go the
anchor.

HAROLD

Harold.

Following the tradition, it would seem that Harold's
ship was driven on the French coast by a storm, though

no attempt is here made to depict a shipwreck. The landing, however, was probably in some way involuntary, as indicated in the following scene.

HIC: APPREHENDIT: WIDO: HAROLDV:

Here Guy seized Harold.

No serious resistance seems to have been made by the English, who are taken prisoners by Guy and his companions. In this scene the fine breed of Norman horses is especially noticeable.

ET DVXIT: EVM AD BELREM: ET IBI EVM: TENVIT:

And led him to Beaurain and there imprisoned him.

We here see Harold's companions led away as captives on foot, though Harold himself is allowed to ride, and is probably the first of the two horsemen, as indicated by his costume. They each have hawks on their fists. Guy probably obliged Harold to ride first, so that he might keep an eye on him while on the way to the castle of Beaurain.

VBI: HAROLD: ꝶWIDO PARABOLANT.

Where Harold and Guy converse.

They have now arrived at the castle and Guy gives an audience to Harold in a vaulted apartment, the con-

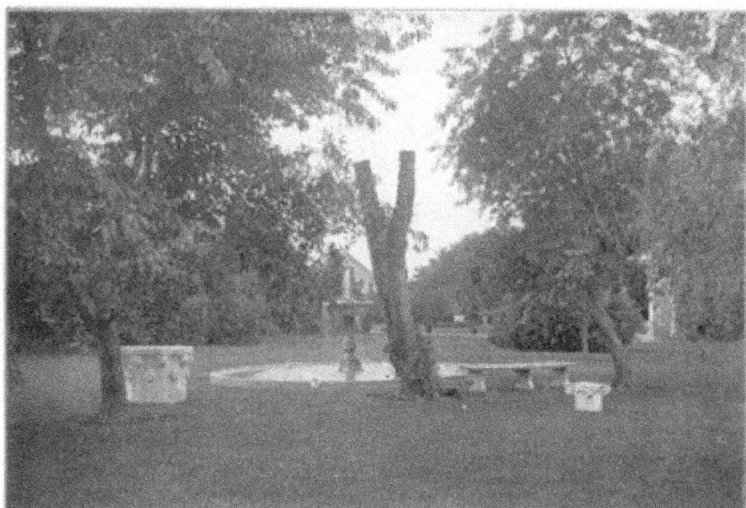

MUSEUM GARDEN LOOKING SOUTHWEST.

struction of which should be noted. The Count is seated
upon his throne with the sword of justice in his hand.
Harold has had his sword restored to him, and also his
attendant. In the midst of the audience a messenger
enters from without, and the reason for his appearance
is shown in the next scene.

VBI: NVNTII: WILHELMI: DVCIS: VENERVNT: AD WIDONE.

Where Duke William's **messengers came to Guy.**

In this and the two following scenes the order of time
is, for some unknown reason, reversed. Here we see
the messengers arriving, in the next they are on their
way, while in the third scene they are about to start.
The messengers are evidently not well received, the
count Guy doubtless taking the ground that his capture of the Englishmen was none of William's business.
We shall see further on, however, that he finally concluded that it would be safer to comply with the Duke's
demand for the release of the prisoners. On the lower
margin of this section is represented an agricultural
scene, comprising ploughing, harrowing and sowing.
A boy driving away birds with a sling will also be
noted. The use of the sling in combat, however, nowhere **appears,** though in more ancient times the

slingers, as well as the archers, were an important
feature in warfare.

TVROLD

Turold.

In the dwarf holding the horses of the messengers on
their way to Beaurain, it has been suggested that we
may have a representation of the designer of the tapestry, though this is guesswork only. In any event, his
beard and shaven head leave no doubt of his Norman
nationality.

NVNTII: WILHELMI

William's Messengers.

This third scene should have been, in the ordinary
sequence, the first of the three scenes here depicted.
The messengers are galloping toward Beaurain, and the
watchman in the tree is probably one of Count Guy's
men in the immediate neighborhood of the castle, who,
in the earlier scene, apprises the count of the arrival of
the messengers.

+ HIC VENIT: NVNTIVS: AD WILHELMVM DVCEM

Here the messenger came to Duke William.

We here see William seated upon his throne, while
his castle at Rouen is represented as a square fortress

flanked with towers. The Duke receives the little messenger who comes to announce the capture of Harold
and his companions by the count Guy, and forthwith
despatches the two knights to demand the release of
Harold.

HIC: WIDO: ADDVXIT HAROLDVM AD **WIL-**
HELMVM: NORMANNORVM: DVCEM.

*Here Guy conducted Harold to William, Duke of the
Normans.*

In this scene we see the result of **William's** demand,
for Guy himself brings Harold, who **now** wears his
spurs, and is accompanied by an armed escort of his
own. The figure of William is worked with unusual
care, and it has been suggested that the designer may
have been a contemporary of William and endeavored
to give as nearly as possible in this kind of work, a
portrait of the Duke.

HIC: DVX: WILGELM: CVM HAROLDO:

VENIT: AD PALATIV SVV

*Here Duke William, together with Harold, came to his
palace.*

In this scene William gives an audience to Harold in
his palace at Rouen. Just what was the nature of the
interview it is impossible to determine, but presumably

Harold delivered his message from king Edward. The
difficulty of interpretation arises from the following
scene, which apparently has no connection with its predecessor, unless their conversation touched in some
way upon Ælfgyva, who now appears as the mysterious
woman in the case.

VBI: VNVS: CLERICVS: ET: ÆLFGYVA

When a certain clerk and Aelfgyva....

This superscription is incomplete, whether by design
or accident it is impossible to determine. In any event
Harold is interested in the lady and learning that she is
at Dol, on the borders of Brittany, and is in danger,
begs William to assist in rescuing her. The request is
readily granted, more particularly as William was about
setting out on an expedition against Conan, count of
Brittany.

This and the following scenes suggest a sort of rude
mediæval Trojan War romance. For an attempt to
unravel the mystery of Aelfgyva the reader is referred
to Mr. Fowke's book on the Tapestry.

HIC: WILLEM: DVX: ET EXERCITVS: EIVS: VENERVNT: AD MONTE MICHAELIS.

*Here Duke William and his army came to Mount
Saint-Michel.*

We have have a view of Mont St. Michel on the
coast of Brittany. In this scene attention is called to

the different styles of military dress. Those with coats
of mail and helmets are the knights. Those in tunics
and caps are the common soldiers. We note here also
the appearance of the cross on William's standard,
though the crusades were not yet under way.

ET HIC: TRANSIERVNT: FLVMEN: COSNONIS.

And here they crossed the River Conesnon.

This river is the boundary between Normandy and
Brittany, and empties into the Bay of Cancale opposite
Mont St. Michel. Here is a shifting quicksand and
the more cautious dismount, and pick their way on
foot, carrying their arms above their heads.

HIC: HAROLD: DVX: TRAHEBAT: EOS: DE ARENA.

Here Duke Harold dragged them out of the quicksand.

Harold was famous for his strength, and is here shown
with one man on his back while he pulls out another,
who is about to be engulfed by the sand. Those re-
ported to have had experience with the quicksands of
Long Island, will particularly appreciate this scene.

ET VENERVNT AD DOL: ET: CONAN: · FVGA VERTIT: ·

And they came to Dol and Conan fled.

The siege of Dol by Conan was apparently unexpected
by William, for his men, galloping up to the walls, are
not in armor.

Conan's soldiers are nevertheless represented as fleeing upon William's approach, possibly anticipating being overpowered by numbers.

REDNES

Rennes.

This was the capital of Brittany where Conan is supposed to have fled to gather reinforcements.

HIC MILITES WILLELMI: DVCIS: PVGNANT: CONTRA DINANTES:· ET: CVNAN: CLAVES: PORREXIT:·

Here Duke William's soldiers fight against the men of Dinan, and Conan reached out the keys.

Here we have an interesting scene representing the attack and repulse of a fortified town in the eleventh century. The Norman soldiers in armor are seen as the attacking party. While the conflict is at its height two knight are seen setting fire to the palisades, which must therefore have been of wood, indicating a very primitive method of defensive walls. The fire may have induced a surrender, for Conan is now seen handing out the keys of the town on a lance, and William receives them in the same manner.

HIC: WILLELM: DEDIT: HAROLDO: ARMA.

*Here **William** gave Harold arms.*

Harold's conduct in the campaign against Conan was evidently highly satisfactory to William, who forthwith knighted him after the affair at Dinan. Harold in this scene is shown holding the banner which has been given him as a symbol of his new dignity.

It may be mentioned here that the defensive armor of the period both in Normandy and England was a combination of leather and steel. The Norman weapons of offence were bows and arrows, a lance, a sword, and the mace. The English on the other hand, made the heavy two-handed battle axe their principal offensive weapon, though they used also the javelin and sword, and, to a limited extent, the bow and arrow. The nose-piece, somewhat after the manner of a modern football team, is also worthy of remark as shown in some of the scenes.

The size and strength of the individual soldier became therefore a most important factor in every encounter. Had the English cultivated the use of the bow and arrow to a greater extent, the result of the battle of Hastings, shortly to be recorded on the tapestry, might have been different.

HIC WILLELM VENIT: BAGIAS VBI HAROLD: SACRAMENTVM: FECIT:· WILHELMO DVCI:·

Here William came to Bayeux where Harold made an oath to Duke William.

The oath of Harold here depicted is one of the best known and oftenest repeated episodes of Harold's mis-

sion to Normandy. There is some doubt as to the
nature of the oath, but the commonly accepted version
is that Harold swore to marry William's daughter, and
give his own sister in marriage to one of the Norman
nobles, and defend William's title to the English crown
upon the death of Eadward. The story runs that William brought a chest filled with the holiest relics and
then covered the chest with a pall. Harold then took
his oath, as shown in the scene, with one hand on the
covered chest, and the other on the altar. After the
oath the pall was removed, upon the order of William, and Harold was made aware of the sacred con-
tents of the chest. Harold, in subsequently breaking
his oath, always claimed that both duress and deceit
had been practised upon him by William. In the tapestry we see the party approaching Bayeux over a
bridge on their way to the place designated for the
ceremony of the oath. On one of the columns of the
nave of the Cathedral at Bayeux is sculptured this
scene of the oath, borrowed from the tapestry.

HIC HAROLD: DVX : · REVERSVS: EST AD
ANGLICAM: TERRAM : ·

Here Duke Harold returned to England.

Having secured the fidelity of Harold so far as lay
in his power, William grants him a safe conduct to
England and we see Harold returning to his native

land, in a ship apparently manned by Norman sailors.
The ship having been signalled, probably at Bosham
manor, the point from which the original party set sail,
the windows of the house are shown filled with gazers,
ready to welcome Harold after his many adventures.
Among others the one upon the balcony is probably
Harold's wife Ealdgyth.

ET VENIT: AD: EDWARDV͞: · REGEM: ·

And came to King Eadward.

Upon disembarking, Harold, sending a messenger
ahead to announce his arrival, proceeds forthwith to
Westminster to report to the king. The latter, represented as enfeebled by age and ill-health, is seated
upon his throne, with his sceptre reversed in his hand,
evidently taking very little interest in terrestrial
affairs.

HIC PORTATVR CORPVS EADWARDI REGIS AD ECCLESIAM SC͞I PETRI AP͞LI

*Here King Eadward's body is carried to the church
of St. Peter the Apostle.*

Here again, as similarly noted in one of the former
scenes, the order of time, for some unexplained reason,
is reversed in the tapestry, so that the burial precedes
the pictorial representation of the last hours and death
of the king. The great lack of proportion among the

objects represented, is especially notable in this scene. The funeral ceremonies are simple enough. The body of the king is borne upon a bier, while boys, ringing bells, walk beside the body, followed by the clergy.

The place of burial, Westminster Abbey, where the remains of the king are still supposed to lie, was at that time called the church of St. Peter the Apostle. The hand issuing from the cloud above, doubtless represents some religious portent indicative of the saintly character of Eadward, for he was afterwards canonized. The large figure of a man, much out of proportion, affixing a weather-cock at the east end of the church, is supposed to suggest the very recent completion of the structure, which had been begun by Eadward himself. The architecture of this church, upon the present site of Westminster Abbey, should be carefully noted.

HIC EADWARDVS: REX IN LECTO : ALLOQVIT: FIDELIS : ·

Here King Eadward, in bed, speaks to his Vassals.

Assuming that Eadward had the right to dispose of the crown of England by nuncupative will, this scene, as affecting the rival claims of Harold and William to the English throne is the most interesting of all. Eadward is upon his death bed, surrounded by English nobles, and the English archbishop Stigand.

One of the English nobles entreats the dying king to designate Harold as his successor. He feebly replies that he has already named Duke William. Then Harold personally urges the king in his own favor. Overcome with the weakness of approaching death, Eadward finally replies: "Let the English make the Duke or Harold king, as they please; I consent."

In considering the legal effect of this scene it would certainly seem that the Norman lawyers could, and doubtless did claim "undue influence" on the part of Harold and his friends.

ET HIC: DEFVNCTVS EST
And here he is dead.

The body is here being prepared for burial. The ecclesiastic is probably the archbishop Stigand.

HIC DEDERVNT HAROLDO CORO·NÅ REGIS.
Here they gave to Harold the crown of the King.

Eadward the Confessor had passed his youth in Normandy, and was in reality more fond of the Normans than the English. For this, and doubtless other reasons, he had originally settled on his cousin William as his successor. The English, however, had no intention of receiving a foreign king in the form of a legacy from a feeble old man. Upon the death of Eadward, therefore, the Assembly forthwith met and proclaimed Harold, their fellow-countryman, king.

The scene here represents a committee of two, appointed by the Witan of England, offering Harold the crown and official axe.

HIC RESIDET: HAROLD REX: ANGLORVM:

Here is seated Harold, King of the English.

Harold is here represented as having been crowned by archbishop Stigand, a fact sufficient in Norman eyes to invalidate his claim, as Stigand's ecclesiastical title was not recognized by the Pope. The coronation takes place in an apartment of the palace at Westminster, and the people are **seen** applauding without.

STIGANT ARCHIEPS

Archbishop Stigand.

The conspicuous position here given in the tapestry to Stigand is probably meant merely to accentuate the invalidity of Harold's title. The archepiscopal see of Canterbury had been bestowed upon Stigand by the king's writ, but Pope Alexander had refused him the pallium. His subsequent investment by Benedict, the anti-pope, had only complicated and embittered the controversy.

ISTI MIRANT STELLA

These men are dismayed at the star.

The appearance of this comet is an historical fact, commented upon by the chronicles of the time. It was supposed to be a portent of the invasion of England.

192 THESE MEN ARE DISMAYED AT HIS SPEAR-HAROLD'S COMER
293 HAROLD
323 HERE AN ENGLISH SHIP CAME INTO THE TERRITORY OF DUKE WILLIAM
Plate 29-31

It is particularly interesting as being the first pictorial representation of a comet that has come down to us, and is now recognized as Halley's Comet.

HAROLD

Harold.

We see here a messenger who brings to Harold a sword. Taken in connection with the ships on the border, this scene may represent, by way of anticipation, news of William's invasion.

HIC: **NAVIS**: ANGLICA: VENIT· IN TERRAM WILLEMI: DVCIS

Here an English ship came into the territory of Duke William.

Eadward's Norman affiliations had induced many nobles of that country to follow him into England. These, doubtless, kept William well informed of all that was going on in England, and this ship may have been chartered by a party of Normans returning to their own country after Eadward's death.

HIC: WILLELM DVX: IVSSIT NAVES: EDIFICARE:

Here Duke William gave orders to build ships.

As soon as William heard of Harold's coronation he lost no time, but began at once his preparations for a descent upon England. The prime necessity for a naval expedition is evidently ships, so these are first attended to, and we here follow their construction from the felling of the trees to their actual launching. In this scene we notice for the first time Bishop Odo, William's half brother. He is designated by his tonsure. He was one of the most active spirits in the whole enterprise, his zeal doubtless stimulated by the thought of the part taken by the heretic archbishop Stigand across the channel.

HIC TRAHVṄT: NAVES: AD MARE :·

Here they drag the ships to the sea.

The size of the ships in the eleventh century evidently did not require any very extensive dockyard facilities, for in these scenes the ships are simply put together on land and then hauled down to the sea. Comparing the date of Harold's coronation with William's descent on England it would seem that the whole preparation for the expedition, including the building and equipment of the fleet, did not require over six or eight months. It is said that William crossed the channel with 3,000 ships and 60,000 men.

ISTI PORTANT: ARMAS: AD NAVES: ET HIC TRAHVNT: CARRV.M CVM VINO: ET ARMIS :·

These men carry arms to the ships, and here they drag a cart with wine and arms.

The custom of regarding wine as a necessary article of subsistence for all classes of the population, which still prevails in France and other European countries, is shown in this scene. The invaders relied on England for food, but knew they must carry their wine with them.

+HIC: WILLELM: DVX IN MAGNO: NAVIGIO: MARE TRANSIVIT ET VENIT AD PEVENESÆ:·

Here Duke William crossed over the sea in a great ship and came to Pevensey.

The expedition set sail from S. Valery-sur-Somme on September 27th, 1066, and in this scene is shown the historic "Mora," the ship presented to William by his wife Matilda. The invasion of England had received the papal sanction, and the reigning Pope, Alexander II presented William with a consecrated banner, which is here seen at the masthead of the "Mora." At the stern is seen the effigy of his little son Rufus, who later, upon the death of his father, ascended the English throne. At nine o'clock on the next morning after setting sail William landed at Pevensey, in Sussex, on the south coast of England, unopposed.

HIC EXEVNT: CABALLI DE NAVIBVS:·

Here the horses go out of the ships.

Even at the present day it is no easy matter to transport horses across the sea, so that the disembarkation of the horses is here properly accorded a place in a separate scene.

ET HIC: MILITES: FESTINAVERVNT: HESTINGA: VT CIBVM . RAPERENTVR:

And here the soldiers hurried on to Hastings to find food.

The appearance of the invaders naturally demoralized the unarmed peasants, who deserted their farms, leaving the oxen, sheep and pigs an easy prey for the Norman soldiers, who proceed to help themselves. We note with interest the use of the lasso by one of the foragers.

HIC EST WADARD

Here is Wadard.

This person is unknown to fame, except for the reference made here in the tapestry. That no mention should have been made of him in any of the chronicles has been advanced as one of the reasons for believing the tapestry to be practically a contemporary work with the scenes it describes. Wadard is here seen taking part in the fun incident to the capture of a small packhorse, connected with which there was doubtless some joke well known to the soldiers, just the sort of thing for a contemporary to introduce into a work of this kind.

HIC: COQVITER: CARO ET HIC: MINISTRAVN MINISTRI:

Here meat is cooked and here the servants serve.

Here we see the result of the successful work of the preceding scenes. The cooks and baker are hard at work and the things are being served on the shields of the soldiers, who have thus improvised a table for the purpose. In accordance with a custom still sometimes practiced in our own country districts, a blast on the horn notifies those at a distance that dinner is ready.

HIC FECERV̄N: PRANDIVM: ET · HIC · EPIS-COPVS: CIB̄V: ET: POT̄V: BENEDICIT:

Here they make a feast, and here the Bishop blesses the food and drink.

Here we see the dinner under full headway at a table in the form of a half circle. There are knives but no forks, the latter being a modern invention. The ecclesiastic asking the blessing is the celebrated Odo,

Bishop of Bayeux, seated on the left of William, his half brother.

ODO: EPS   WILLELM :·
ROTBERT:

Bishop Odo. William. Robert.

The three are holding a counsel of war. Odo is the speaker and the result of their deliberations is shown in the following scene:

ISTE · IVSSIT: VT FODERETVR: CASTELLVM: AT · HESTENGA.

The latter commanded that a rampart **should be** *thrown up* **at** *Hastings.*

ISTE refers to Robert of Mortain, the last name among the three embroidered in the preceding scene. He it is who looks after the details of the work. It will be noticed that the spades have only one tread for the foot.

CEASTRA.

The camp.

We see the fort on the mound that has been thrown up. This fort is probably of wood and has been brought

over from Normandy, for such portable strongholds
were common at that time.

HIC: NVNTIATVM EST: WILLELM DE HAR-OLD:

Here tidings are brought to William of Harold.

We here see William seated, with the consecrated
banner in his hand, listening to the story of an armed
knight, who is doubtless telling him of Harold's great
victory in the north over the Norwegians, allies of the
Normans, headed by Tosti, Harold's rebellious brother.

HIC DOMVS INCENDITVR

Here a house is burnt.

Previous to the actual engagement it would seem
from this that some excesses were committed.

HIC: MILITEs: EXIERVNT: DE HESTENGA: ET: VENERVNT AD PRELIVM: CONTRA: HAROLDVM: REGE :

*Here the Knights left Hastings and came to give
battle to King Harold.*

William comes forth from Hastings and puts himself
at the head of his army. Accompanying him is a
knight, together with two standard bearers, one carrying the consecrated banner, of which so much is natur-

ally made, and the other a banner which is supposed to represent the celebrated Black Raven of the Danes.

HIC: WILLELM: DVX INTERROGAT: VITAL: SI VIDISSET HAROLDI EXERCITV :

Here Duke William asks Vital if he had seen the army of Harold.

Vital is evidently one of a returning scouting party, and his gestures, in replying to William's question, indicate that he and his soldiers had seen the English army.

ISTE NVNTIAT: HAROLDVM REGE DE EXERCITV WILELMI

One informs King Harold concerning the army of Duke William.

Harold had taken up his position on the Hill of Senlac, and also sends out scouts to learn of the position of William's army. We here see one of the spies taking observations from a hill and then reporting to Harold.

HIC   WILLELM   DVX   ALLOQVITVR   SVIS MILITIBVS VT PREPARAREN SE VIRILITER ET   SAPIENTER   AD   PRELIVM   CONRA ANGLORVM EXERCITV.

Here Duke William exhorts his soldiers to prepare themselves manfully and discreetly for the battle against the army of the English.

The battle is now about to begin. The policy of Harold in risking everything in this one battle had

been much criticized by his brother Gyrth, who urged
him to harass the enemy and wear them out by delays,
the English having the great advantage of being in
their own country, and therefore able to obtain re-en-
forcements from time to time. Harold, however, doubtless flushed with his recent victory over the Norwegians, was determined to hazard everything, and had
previously declared that he would either be the victor
in this one fight or die in the attempt to maintain his
throne. The archers, who were such a prominent feature on the Norman side, preceded the cavalry and the
battle is begun by a flight of arrows. The mounted
knights then rush forward, but are met by the interlocked shields of the English phalanx standing shoulder
to shoulder. Harold, surrounded by his standard
bearer and his four brothers, is seen wielding his
famous two-handed battle axe. The incidents of the
fight now begin to be depicted on the border of the
tapestry.

HIC CECIDERVNT LEWINE ET: GẎRD: FRATRES: HAROLDI REGIS.

*Here fell Leofwine and Gyrth, brothers of King
Harold.*

In this scene are shown Harold and his brothers making a stand against the Normans. In the encounter
the two brothers above mentioned are killed, leaving
Harold with his battle axe to contend alone. As men-

tioned above, it was Gyrth who advised against risking everything on the issue of a single battle.

HIC CECIDERVN SIMVL: ANGLI ET FRANCI: IN PRELIO.

Here English and French fell at the same time in battle.

Here we have the climax of the fight. The Normans had been repulsed, or, according to one account, had purposely retreated as though overpowered, in order to deceive the English, only to rally suddenly and turn upon their pursuers.

HIC. ODO EPS: BACVLV. TENENS CONFOR: · TAT PVEROS.

Here Bishop Odo, holding a club, rallies the young troops.

The activity of the upper clergy in the actual fighting, both on the Norman and English side, was one of the features of the conflict, only following, however, the custom of the time. By the word "PVEROS" is probably meant those who were having their first actual experience of war.

HIC EST: · WILEL DVX: ·

Here is Duke William.

It appears, according to the chroniclers, that at one time a report was spread abroad that Duke William had been killed, and a panic was about to ensue among the Normans. Hearing of this report William hurried to the front and, raising his helmet and showing himself to his troops, exclaimed: "I am here," or perhaps made use of the actual words of the inscription:

E....TIVS.

Eustace.

During the above scene Eustace, Count of Boulogne, was at William's side, and he seems to have been of sufficient importance in the battle to accord him separate mention in the tapestry.

HIC: FRANCI PVGNAN ET CECIDERVNT QVI ERANT: CVM HAROLDO:·

Here the French fight and those who were with Harold fell.

This scene shows that the Normans had practically won the day, and just at this time William gave his celebrated order, "Shoot *upwards,* Norman archers." The border here illustrates this feature of the fight. The shield-wall of the English was of no avail against the falling arrows and demoralization quickly followed.

HIC HAROLD:· REX:· INTERFECTVS: EST.

Here King Harold was slain.

It was while still bravely wielding his axe that, following the chroniclers, a falling arrow pierced Harold

in the eye. Seeking to pluck it out the shaft broke in
his grasp and the English king fell mortally wounded.
With the death of Harold the battle is over and William becomes master of England.

ET FVGA: VERTERVN ANGLI.

And the English fled.

It has been conjectured that the original tapestry was
still further continued by additional scenes so as to
include the coronation of William. If this be true,
there is at the present time no record of that fact, and
for us the story of the tapestry is told with the defeat
of the English at the battle of Hastings.

THE ROYAL EFFIGIES.

SOUTH SIDE OF THE MUSEUM.

THE ROYAL EFFIGIES.

The royal effigies, in half length, here exhibited at Southampton, are copies from electrotype reproductions now in the possession of the National Portrait Gallery at London. The original electrotype copies were made about twenty-five years ago from moulds taken from the effigies themselves, which in full length, made either in bronze, metal, alabaster or marble, lie recumbent upon the royal tombs in Westminster Abbey and Canterbury Cathedral.

The plaster copies here shown, made with the kind permission of the trustees of the National Portrait Gallery, are, curiously enough, considering the interest of the effigies, the only copies that have ever been taken from the original electrotype reproductions. The following **is** a list, in historical sequence, of the effigies and portrait busts of these Plantagenet and Tudor kings and queens, with one or two affiliated royal personages, with the dates of their birth and death:

Henry III.........................1207–1272
Eleanor of Castile..................1245–1290
Edward III........................1312–1377
Edward, "The Black Prince" (the
   only electrotype copy in this col-
   lection) 1330–1376
Richard II.........................1366–1400
Henry IV..........................1366–1413
"The Lady Margaret," countess of
   Richmond (mother of Henry VII.).1441–1509
Henry VII.........................1456–1509
Elizabeth of York (wife of Henry VII.)1466–1502
Portrait bust of Henry VIII........1491–1547
Queen Elizabeth....................1533–1603
Portrait bust of Mary Stuart, Queen
   of Scots..........................1542–1587

HENRY III.
(1207-1272.)
Page 47.

HENRY III.

(1207–1272.)

Henry III., called of Winchester, was the son
of king John of England and Isabella of Angou-
lême. He came to the throne upon the death of his
father, and ten days after that event, at the age of
nine, was crowned at Gloucester, October 28, 1216. He
was king for fifty-six years, the third longest reign in
English history, being exceeded only by those of
George III. and Victoria. During Henry's minority,
under the guidance of able counsellors, England en-
joyed a period of comparative peace, in marked contrast to the confusion and turmoil of his father's reign.
The GREAT CHARTER, extorted by the Barons from
king John at Runnymede in 1215, was enlarged in its
scope and confirmed. In the earlier days of English
history, the character of the sovereign, as affecting the
peace and prosperity of the people, was of the utmost

importance, and as Henry grew up it was discovered, with ever-increasing alarm, that he had none of the qualities of a ruler. Hampered by the provisions of the Great Charter, he endeavored to throw off its restraints, and hence arose the Barons' War, wherein the rights and liberties of the people were championed by Simon de Montfort, earl of Leicester. It is to Simon de Montfort (more than to any other individual of those early times) that the English-speaking race owes its initiation into the form and substance of popular government, for it was he who, in 1265, having defeated the forces of the king, summoned the first Parliament that the people (though that word is used in a restricted sense) had any real share in electing.

Henry III. was a feeble, extravagant, irresolute king. He died in 1272 at the age of sixty-five. "He was as much a king in death as he had ever been in life. He was the mere pale shadow of a king at all times."

The original full-length effigy in bronze, of which this is a half-length copy in plaster, is a recumbent figure upon his tomb in the chapel of Edward the Confessor, in Westminster Abbey.

ELEANOR OF CASTILE.

(1245-1290.)

Eleanor of Castile, wife of Edward I., was the daughter of Ferdinand III., king of Castile. At the time of the

ELEANOR OF CASTILE.
(1245-1290.)
Page 48.

death of his father, Henry III., in 1272, Edward (born at Westminster in 1239) was away in the Holy Land on a crusade, accompanied by his popular and accomplished wife, and did not return to England until two years after he became king. Arriving in England by way of Italy, in 1274, at the age of thirty-six, he was received with enthusiasm by the whole people who were proud of their knightly king (it was the height of the age of chivalry), who had acquired great distinction by his conduct in the Holy War in the East, and he and his queen were forthwith crowned with magnificence in Westminster Abbey.

A resolute monarch, Edward I. introduced many reforms, and, ruling England with a firm hand for thirty-five years, extended his kingdom so as to embrace Wales and most of Scotland. The wars with Scotland developed the character of Sir William Wallace, who has remained down to our own day, the typical hero of his country. After an heroic resistance he was captured and brought to England, and executed as an outlaw.

Just after Wales was subdued, queen Eleanor gave birth, in the Welsh castle of Carnarvon, to a son, and the king, showing him to the Welsh people as one of their fellow-countrymen, called him Prince of Wales, thus fulfilling his promise that one of their own countrymen who could speak neither French nor English should rule over them. At least so the story runs.

This prince, his elder brothers having died before him, after the death of his father, became Edward II. of England. Ever since this episode the heir to the English throne has been known as the Prince of Wales.

Following and preceding the disastrous reigns of his father and son respectively, the reign of Edward I., from the point of view of national development, represents a bright page in English history.

One of the earlier English historians thus describes the queen, incidentally mentioning the nine crosses that were erected to her memory: "To our nation she was a loving mother, the column and pillar of the whole realm; therefore to her glory, the king her husband caused all those famous trophies to be erected, wherein her noble corse did rest; for he loved her above all earthly creatures. She was a godly, modest, and merciful princess; the English nation in her time was not harassed by foreigners, nor the country people by the purveyors of the crown. The sorrow-stricken she consoled as became her dignity, and she made them friends who were at discord."[*]

---

[*] Of the crosses one was set up where the Charing Cross Railway Station now stands, near Trafalgar Square in London (Chère Reine₊). The official and court language of England was French up to the time of Edward III. when the great English victories over the French made the English language popular, even among the descendants of the old Norman nobility, and by act of Parliament all pleadings in the law courts were from that time on conducted in English. The poetry of Chaucer and the appearance of Wycliffe's translation of the bible had also doubtless much to do with popularizing the change among the upper class, for both were widely read by them, and our language then began to assume the literary form it has since retained.

Queen Eleanor died in 1290, and the full-length effigy
in gilt bronze, of which this is in part a plaster copy,
was made in London by William Torel, an Englishman, in 1291, and is a recumbent figure upon her
tomb in the chapel of Edward the Confessor in Westminster Abbey. Near her lies her husband, whose tomb
is without an effigy. Their son, Edward II., succeeded
to the throne at the age of twenty-three, upon the death
of his father in 1307. After a miserable reign he was
deposed and murdered, and was succeeded by his son,
Edward III.

"If you ever come near Gloucester, and see the
centre tower of its beautiful cathedral, with its four
rich pinnacles rising lightly in the air, you may remember that the wretched Edward II. lies buried in the
old Abbey of that ancient city, at forty-three years old,
after being for nineteen and a half years a perfectly
incapable king."

EDWARD III.

(1312-1377.)

Edward III was born at Windsor and ascended the
throne at the age of fourteen upon the deposition of his
father, Edward II, in 1327.

At the age of sixteen he married Philippa, daughter

of the count of Hainault, reputed to be the hand-
somest young woman of her time, and their eldest son
was the celebrated Edward, "The Black Prince."

During the reign of Edward III occurred the battles
of Crécy (1346) and Poitiers (1356), in both of which
the English, led by the Black Prince, with forces
greatly inferior in number to the French, inflicted upon
the latter disastrous defeats. To this day, among the
French, Crécy and Poitiers and the later Agincourt
(1415) have left their sting.

Regarded from the point of view of military success
in her many wars with France, the reign of Edward
III marks the culmination of England's glory, rivalled
only by that of Henry V.

In domestic affairs occurred many events which mark
this period as one of the sad reigns in English history,
so far as the condition of the people was concerned. In
1348 appeared the terrible scourge known as the "Black
Death." Beginning in China, this extraordinary pes-
tilence devastated Europe from the shores of the
Mediterranean to the Baltic, and, swooping down upon
England like a cyclone, is conjectured to have dimin-
ished the population by one-half, so that between 1350
and 1370 there were probably not more than a couple
of millions of people in all England. The destruction
of so large a proportion of the laboring class produced
the greatest misery and confusion, and attempts to
remedy the attendant evils by legislation fixing the
price of labor seemed only to add to the difficulties of

EDWARD III.
(1312-1377.)
Page 51.

the situation, thus laying the foundation for the
Peasants' Revolt of the following reign, one of the
great historic conflicts between capital and labor.

In capacity for government, Edward ranks as one of
the few great kings of England. As a financier, both in
public and private affairs, he was tricky and dishonest,
repudiating without scruple his obligations to parliament, when money had been granted on certain conditions, and by coolly refusing to pay his just debts was
known to have forced into bankruptcy many of the domestic and foreign bankers who had loaned him money.
In his diplomatic negotiations with foreign princes, this
underlying falseness of character was also conspicuous.
But as a successful commander in the field, and a dominating spirit in the conduct of affairs of State, he
made himself respected by the turbulent baronage,
ever ready to take advantage of any evidence of weakness on the part of their sovereign. In manners he was
affable and obliging, knowing how to make himself
agreeable to all ranks of society, and equally at home
at a merchants' dinner in London or at a knightly
tournament surrounded by the glitter of the court,
of which he was very fond. In disposition he had a
certain superficial generosity, though at times liable to
be swayed by the violence of his passions, as shown in
his intended treatment of the six burghers of Calais,
who were saved from an ignominious and unmerited
death only through the interposition of his queen.
Following and preceding the feeble reigns of his father

and grandson respectively, the English are justly proud
of this period in their history, so far as the accomplish-
ment of results was concerned effected through the
talents and ability of their sovereign. The life of the
court was one of lavish display and magnificence, so
far as the condition of the country permitted, and
though the real spirit of chivalry was dead, a brave
attempt was made to keep up appearances.

The later years of Edward III were clouded by mis-
fortune. His mental faculties partly gave way and
the feeble old man was but a wreck of his former self,
falling entirely under the influence of Alice Perrers,
a handsome and spirited woman, clever enough to
require the intervention of parliament to put a stop to
her intriguing activity in the affairs of the court and
government. Edward's incapacity at this period of his
life had, however, its bright side, for the disorders of
the kingdom were such that parliament came more
and more to the front, so that substantial progress
was made in the direction of constitutional government.

The appearance of John Wycliffe and Geoffrey
Chaucer, whose services in their respective spheres are
touched upon in the account of the following reign,
were events of the greatest importance. In this reign,
also, appeared William Longland, familiarly known as
"Long Will," the sad poet of the people, voicing their
sorrows and sense of degradation in his quaint and dolor-
ous poem of "Piers the Ploughman," the very counter-

EDWARD,
"THE BLACK PRINCE"
(1330-1376.)
Page 55.

part of the "Canterbury Tales" of the courtly
Chaucer. An interesting figure also is John Ball,
"the mad priest of Kent," as Froissart calls him, who
for twenty years preached the natural equality of man,
and by his homely eloquence stirred among the people
an intense longing for a betterment of their social condition.

Of the minor events of this period the building of
Windsor Castle is one of the most interesting, together
with the establishment of the knightly Order of the
Garter, membership in which, down to our own day, is
the most coveted distinction in English social and
political life. At this time also the English language
was substituted for the French in all legal proceedings.

Edward III died in 1377, and was quietly succeeded
by his grandson, Richard II.

The full length effigy, of which this is in part a plaster copy, is a recumbent figure, in bronze, upon his
tomb in the chapel of Edward the Confessor in Westminster Abbey. It was apparently taken from a death
mask, as indicated by the closed eyes and the appearance of the beard.

EDWARD " THE BLACK PRINCE."

(1330-1376.)

This heroic figure in English history was the eldest
son of Edward III and Philippa of Hainault. At the

age of thirty-one he married his cousin Joan, commonly known as "The Fair Maid of Kent," though at the
time of her marriage she had already been twice a widow.
Their only son was the ill-fated Richard II, and with
his death in 1400 this branch of the royal family disap-
pears from history. As the great warrior of his time
and the vanquisher of the French in the battles of
Crécy (1346) and Poitiers (1356) the "Black Prince"
has left a name and fame rivalled among English
princes only by that of Henry V, whom in many respects
he much resembled. With the exception of certain measures of excessive harshness committed in the heat of
war, he displayed throughout his brilliant career great
self-command and moderation in the hour of victory.

His personal courage and genius as a commander, in
an age of ever-recurring war, made him the most conspicuous leader of his time, and his brilliant victories
over the great armies of France with his little bands of
English archers brought him a renown that in no way
fades with time. In disposition he was generous and
magnanimous, in manners affable and pleasing, and he
is still revered as the great Englishman of those
troubled times. He died in 1376, a year before his
father and so never came to the throne.

With the weakening of his father's faculties toward
the close of the king's life, the intelligence and character of the "Black Prince," though himself a confirmed invalid, were of the greatest importance in shap-
ing the policy of the government in the public interest.

RICHARD II.
(1366-1400.)
Page 57.

The original full length effigy in alabaster, of which this in part is an electrotype copy, is a recumbent figure upon his tomb in Canterbury cathedral. An ancient coat of mail, a helmet, and a pair of gauntlets he is supposed to have worn, are suspended above the tomb.

RICHARD II.

(1366-1400.)

Richard II was the son of Edward, the "Black Prince" and Joan of Kent, and ascended the throne in 1377, at the age of eleven, upon the death of his grandfather, Edward III. At the age of sixteen he married Anne of Bohemia, of the same age as himself, daughter of Charles IV, Emperor of Germany, a very amiable and pious young woman, greatly esteemed by the people, among whom she was known as the "good queen Anne." She died in 1394 at the age of twenty-eight. A year or two later Richard married the little Isabel, daughter of Charles VI of France, only eight years old at the time of her marriage, the king being about thirty. Isabel was the older sister of Catharine, who afterward married Henry V of England.

At the time of Richard's accession the most powerful and influential men in the kingdom were his three uncles, the dukes of Lancaster (John of Gaunt), York, and Gloucester, younger brothers of the "Black Prince," and they managed for a time to get along reasonably

well together in the conduct of the government during
the king's minority. But in that rude age the power
and turbulence of the feudal nobility were pretty certain to create trouble, unless restrained by a strong
hand, and Richard from his youth, inexperience, and
character was entirely incapable of the task imposed
upon him by his position. The record of this reign is,
therefore, largely made up of turmoil and civil com-
motion.

In 1381 occurred the so-called Peasants' Revolt, the
foundation for which had been laid in the previous
reign, headed by Wat Tyler, Jack Straw and other
desperate leaders determined at the risk of their lives
to better the condition of the laboring class.

The rapacity and oppression of the nobility had reduced the people to a state of poverty and wretched-
ness, and unable longer to endure their miserable condition they rose in rebellion. A hundred thousand of
them collected at Blackheath and demanded reforms,
showing a particular animosity against lawyers and
attorneys, and they proceeded to cut off the heads of
such members of this learned profession and others of
their well-to-do fellow subjects as they could lay their
hands on. During a lull in these proceedings, Richard,
happening to pass through Smithfield, very slenderly
guarded, unexpectedly met Tyler at the head of a band
of rioters, and invited him to confer in regard to
the trouble. The latter accepted the invitation,
and directing his companions to remain some

distance behind, rode into the midst of the king's retinue, leaving word with his friends, however, that at a given signal they were to follow him, and murder the whole company, except the king, who was to be taken prisoner. During the conference Tyler seems to have borne himself with great rudeness toward the king, for one Walworth, mayor of London, incensed at his conduct, suddenly struck him, and he was killed on the spot by the king's men, before the eyes of his companions. At once appreciating the danger of the situation for himself and his followers, young Richard, being only sixteen years of age, of his own motion, rode forward at once alone into the midst of the angry mob and with entire self-possession and in a conciliatory manner asked: "What is the meaning of all this disorder, my good people? Are ye angry that ye have lost your leader? I am your king; I will be your leader." The courage and resolution of the handsome boy, the son of their heroic prince, whose memory was still green in the hearts of all classes of Englishmen, had the most extraordinary effect. They followed him into the fields outside the city, where promises were made and charters given them in fulfilment of their demands. Needless to add the charters and promises ultimately proved but delusions, for the social evils of that period were too deeply rooted to be cured offhand.

After this episode it seemed as though England were to be again ruled with a firm hand, but such was not to be. As Richard grew up, the weak side of his character began to develop, for he seems to have been a curious combination of indolence and irresolution on the one hand, set off at times with an unexpected energy, strength, and courage. Surrounded during his youth by a set of grasping politicians, led on different sides by his intriguing uncles, his education in essentials had been greatly neglected, and he grew up a very unbalanced young man, with a violent temper, lacking in judgment and stability, lavish in expense, and fond of show. His manner of living indicated his character. His household is reputed to have consisted of ten thousand persons, with three hundred employed in the kitchen alone. To keep up such an establishment entailed, of course, an enormous expense, and the burden of entertaining this standing army of luxurious idlers could ultimately fall only upon the people themselves. Hence, doubtless, with other causes, arose Wat Tyler's rebellion, and the numerous public discontents that were a feature of this unfortunate reign.

Of the dramatic events in the life of the court the most interesting was the quarrel between the duke of Norfolk and the duke of Hereford (afterward duke of Lancaster, and later Henry IV). It was an affair of honor between the two noblemen—the words "liar" and "traitor" having passed between them—and they arranged to settle their differences by a personal encounter according to the laws of the then waning chivalry. The affair was to come off at Coventry in the presence of the king and a parliamentary committee appointed for the purpose, together with all the nobility and gentry of England who could manage to attend, and, as attendance at the event was also open to all, we may be sure there was no lack of spectators. In fact all England was on the tiptoe of expectation. Just as the duel was about to begin, the king, by the advice of the parliamentary committee and doubtless much to the chagrin and disappointment of the assembled crowd, intervened and decreed exile for both the dukes, Norfolk for life and Hereford for ten years, afterwards reduced to six in consideration of Henry's behavior. This scene is finely treated in Shakespeare's play of Richard II.

During Hereford's enforced absence, his father, John of Gaunt, died, and in violation of a promise, the king declared the duke's vast estates forfeited to the crown. Angered by this breach of faith, Hereford, now Henry, duke of Lancaster, sailed for England to lay claim to his inheritance. Landing at Ravenspur, in Yorkshire, he was agreeably surprised to find himself the most popular man in England, and began secretly to entertain the hope of deposing his cousin the king, and placing himself upon the throne. Richard, not appreciating the danger of his position, had indiscreetly gone to Ireland to avenge the death of another cousin, the earl of March, grandson of Lionel, duke of Clarence, and heir to the throne; and Henry's cause gained such headway during the king's absence that upon his

hasty return, all hope of regaining his authority had
to be given up. Being taken prisoner Richard was
brought to London, and having resigned his title to the
crown in favor of Henry, the latter, as Henry IV,
ascended the throne peaceably, with the approval both
of parliament and the people at large, for Richard's
conduct of the government had alienated from him all
classes of his subjects.*

---

*The manner in which Richard II was deposed and Henry IV
ascended the throne, has in it so much of the element of drama, and is
so indicative of the character of the times, that the following short
account cannot fail to be read with interest.

Parliament being assembled with all the turbulent feudal barons in
their places, as well as the upper clergy and members of the House of
Commons, thirty-three articles of impeachment, recounting the various
crimes and derelictions of Richard, were read. Of all the assembled
notables one man alone stood up to defend the king. In a noble and
forceful speech the Bishop of Carlisle pointed out the dangers incident
to the deposition of their lawful sovereign. No sooner had he finished
than he was at once arrested, by order of Henry, and committed to
prison. The articles were then passed unanimously and the throne
declared vacant, whereupon Henry stepped forth and, with his hand
upon the throne, crossed himself upon the forehead and breast, and
calling upon the name of Christ, pronounced the following words which
are here given in the exact language used by the duke, being an interesting specimen of our language as written about the time of the death
of Chaucer:

*In the name of Fadher, Son and Holy Ghost, I Henry of Lancaster,
challenge this rewme of Ynglande, and the crown, with all the membres
and appurtenances; als that I am descendit by right line of the blode,
coming fro the gude King Henry therde and throge that right that God
of his grace hath sent me, with help of kyn, and of my frendes to
recover it; the which rewme was in poynt to be ondone by defaut of
governance, and ondoying of the gude laws.*

The above suggestion of hereditary title was founded on an idle tale,
believed by no intelligent Englishman, that the eldest son of Henry III
was Edmond, earl of Lancaster, surnamed Crouchback, and not Edward
I. Henry IV, through the female line, was descended from Edmond and

Regarded from the point of view of constitutional development this reign is an important one in English history. The authority of parliament was greatly increased and the deposition of a lawful king, for unlawful acts, followed by the seating of another upon the throne, is in some respects analogous to a similar exercise of power at the time of the revolution of 1688, when James II was, by act of parliament, replaced by William III.

This period is, moreover, made illustrious by the fame of two men, whose best work was done during Richard's reign. In the religious world appeared John Wycliffe, the great reformer, whose translation of the Bible laid the foundation for modern English prose, and Geoffrey Chaucer, whose "Canterbury Tales" entitle him to rank as the father of modern English poetry.

Directly or indirectly through queen Anne, herself a friend and supporter of Wycliffe, and a devout reader of his bible, the latter's writings became known in Bohemia and John Huss, the son of a peasant, stirred by the English preacher, appeared as the forerunner of the reformation in Germany. In England Wycliffe's writings had a far-reaching influence among all classes of the people.

---

had the tale been true would have been rightful heir to the throne. The circumstances were then such, however, that no one thought fit to question Henry's challenge to the crown, and the superior claim of the young earl of March being passed over in silence, the duke of Lancaster seated himself upon the vacant throne and, amid the acclamations of the assembled parliament, assumed the title of Henry IV.

Richard's end was a very sad one. By act of parliament he was ordered to be confined in strict seclusion at Pontefract Castle, and a few months after his deposition, at the age of thirty-four, was there murdered. Some say he was hacked to death by his guards. Others that he was starved to death. The truth can never be known. He left no posterity.

He was originally buried at Langley, but in after years Henry V gave him a royal resting place in Westminster Abbey, in the chapel of Edward the Confessor, where his body now lies.

The original metal gilt full length effigy, of which this, in part, is a plaster copy, lies recumbent upon his tomb by the side of that of his first wife, Anne of Bohemia. As the work was done during the life of the king, about four years before his death, there is every reason to believe that the effigy is a good likeness, particularly as it accords with his portrait, painter unknown, now in the possession of the National Portrait Gallery at London.

HENRY IV.

(1366-1413.)

Henry IV., called of Bolingbroke, the first of the Lancastrian kings, was the son of John of Gaunt (fourth son of Edward III) and Blanche,

HENRY IV.
(1366-1413.)
Page 64.

daughter of Henry, duke of Lancaster. Although Henry had no hereditary title to the throne, the people at large quietly acquiesced in his accession as the most practical way of replacing Richard II, and the character and abilities of Henry enabled him to sustain his position.

The active part played by the parliament which assembled in 1399 to take into account the disordered state of the kingdom, the result of Richard's inability to govern, gave to that body a dignity and importance not previously attained by it in English history.

Henry IV, though claiming the throne by right of descent from Henry III, and also by right of conquest, was in reality fully alive to the weakness of those claims, and practically recognized that the real strength of his title was founded on the consent of the people represented in parliament, though that body was at that time far from being the popular assembly it has since become. During the reign of Henry IV, England, for the above and other reasons, was more of a constitutional monarchy than she had ever been before, or was destined to be again, for many generations after his death.

Henry was a resolute monarch, uniting, with his resolution, craft and caution, qualities pre-eminently requisite, considering the times in which he lived, and the circumstances under which he acquired the crown, to maintain him in his position. He died in 1413 at the age of forty-seven after a reign of fourteen years, and was succeeded by his famous son, Henry V.

He lies buried in Canterbury Cathedral, where his full-length effigy in alabaster (sculptor unknown) of which this is in part a plaster copy, lies recumbent upon his tomb.

For the dramatic treatment of this interesting period of English history, see Shakespeare's Richard II, Henry IV, and Henry V.

MARGARET BEAUFORT, "THE LADY MARGARET."

(1441-1509.)

Margaret Beaufort, countess of Richmond and Derby, was the mother of Henry VII, and through her he obtained such shadowy hereditary title as he had to the English throne. She was the great grand-daughter of John of Gaunt, duke of Lancaster (fourth son of Edward III), the father of Henry IV. Her father was John Beaufort, duke of Somerset, son of John, earl of Somerset, son of John of Gaunt and Catharine Swynford (sister-in-law of the poet Chaucer). The bar sinister was however a blot upon the escutcheon of Margaret's grandfather, the earl of Somerset. John of Gaunt, later in life, married Catharine, and at his earnest solicitation, his nephew, Richard II, obtained the passage of an act of parliament, sanctioned by the Pope, legitimating his children. The effect of this act, with a certain amendment thereto, passed in the reign

MARGARET BEAUFORT.
"THE LADY MARGARET."
(1441-1509.)
Page 66.

of Henry IV, as bearing upon the succession to the crown, was much disputed by the lawyers of the time when the question became a vital one as affecting the claim of Henry VII to represent the Lancastrian faction in its struggle for the possession of the throne. Although there were other descendants of John of Gaunt whose title was genealogically preferable to that of Henry, they were foreigners, and Englishmen were not yet prepared, as in the time of the Georges, to go outside of England for a king. Thus it happened that Henry, being the only available candidate, was finally accepted, and upon his promise to marry Elizabeth of York, in the event of his accession, he gained also many valuable adherents from the followers of the fortunes of the house of York, though the weak points in his genealogical armor, both on his father's and mother's side, were savagely attacked, in very blunt English, in Richard's proclamation calling upon his subjects to repel the invader.* Margaret

---

*It must be acknowledged that from the point of view of royal descent Henry VII cuts but a sorry figure in the presence of a Plantagenet king. Though counting among his progenitors a king of France as well as of England, the royal strain had been so diluted that the feudal baronage could not but regard him as something in the nature of an upstart, forced upon them by political conditions. Consciousness of the low estimation in which his pedigree was held by the old nobility had doubtless much to do with his hatred of the Yorkists, and presumably also with his dislike of his wife, of whose position as rightful heir to the crown he was always exceedingly jealous. When securely seated upon the throne he began to furbish up his paternal ancestry, in a spirit not unknown to the modern genealogist in humbler walks of life, and claimed royal descent through a line of Welsh princes for his Tudor grandfather, not stopping in his ambitious flight until he had reached the half mythical Arthur, that British king around whom cling so many

Beaufort married Edmund Tudor, son of Owen Tudor
and Catharine of Valois, widow of Henry V of England. Owen Tudor was a handsome Welshman, of ob-
scure origin, and had fought in the ranks at the battle
of Agincourt. Being brought to the attention of
Henry V, the king had employed him about the court
where he made the acquaintance of the queen. After
Henry's death Catharine retired to private life and very
little is then known of her. Though no record exists
to prove the fact, she is supposed to have been secretly
married to Owen Tudor, and her sons were treated with
consideration by their half brother, Henry VI, for it
was he who created Edmund, the eldest, earl of Richmond.† Margaret was only thirteen when she was
married to the young earl and was left a widow at the age
of about fourteen, a couple of months before the birth of
Henry. Throughout her long life she subordinated
everything to advancing the interests of her son, who,

---

legends celebrated in the story and song of the elder as well as later
times, and forming such a conspicuous feature in the poetry of our own
day in the flowing verse of Tennyson. To accentuate his esteem for his
alleged though unproved royal British ancestry, at least so far as any
records show, Henry's eldest son was named for the hero of the Knights
of the Round Table, and it was Arthur who became the first husband
of the unfortunate Catharine of Aragon. This marriage entailed
momentous consequences for the English speaking race, for it was the
pretended scruples of Henry VIII in having married his brother's
widow that led to the divorce of Catharine, so fruitful of results in
separating the Church of England from the Church of Rome.

†For a very interesting account of the life and death of Owen Tudor,
including an inquiry into his doubtful antecedents, with references to
authors and documents of the period, see Agnes Strickland's "Katharine
of Valois" in her "Lives of the Queens of England."

from his childhood till he ascended the throne, was
reared in an atmosphere of hardship, danger, and priva-
tion, and disciplined in the rough school of adversity.
As he himself told one of his friends he had always
been, from the age of five till his accession, either a
prisoner or a fugitive. It was during these weary years
of captivity, when he was thrown upon his own re-
sources for amusement, that he acquired the habit of
reading, which gave him a certain reflective tone that
distinguished him in after years.

"The Lady Margaret" was the most notable English-
woman of her time. She was the founder of St. John's
College and of Christ's College at Cambridge, and
established professorships of divinity both at Oxford
and Cambridge. A woman of strong, as well as amiable character, there existed between her and her
youthful grandson, afterward Henry VIII, a genuine
attachment, and when Henry came to the throne he
relied greatly upon her experience and generally recognized sound judgment in the selection of his ministers,
thus giving the people an excellent impression of his
own good sense.

Margaret Beaufort was three times married, her
third husband being Lord Stanley, afterwards earl of
Derby, the man who deserted Richard at a critical
moment in the battle of Bosworth and turned the day
in favor of his step-son. It was Stanley who picked up
Richard's crown on the battle field, and placing it on

Henry's head, led in the acclaim of the earl as Henry VII, King of England.

Margaret Beaufort died in 1509, outliving but a short time her own royal son.

The half-length figure here shown is in part a plaster copy of the full length effigy, in bronze, which lies recumbent upon her tomb in the chapel of Henry VII in Westminster Abbey.

The original is the work of Pietro Torregiano.

HENRY VII.

(1456-1509.)

Henry VII ascended the throne in the year 1485 at the age of twenty-nine. His paternal grandfather was Owen Tudor, a Welsh clansman, who married Catharine, daughter of Charles VI of France, and widow of Henry V of England, the "Kate" in Shakespeare's play of Henry V. The son of this marriage, Edmund Tudor, earl of Richmond, married "The Lady Margaret," as she was called, a great granddaughter of John of Gaunt, duke of Lancaster, fourth son of Edward III. The house of York was descended, through the female line, from Lionel, duke of Clarence, third son of Edward III, and the disputes between these two branches of the royal house of Plantagenet unsettled England, off and on, for over a hundred years. Owing to the fact that the

HENRY VII.
(1456-1509.)
Page 70.

first and second sons of Edward III left no descendants,
with the exception of the deposed Richard II, there
was no question but that the legal title of the house of
York was superior to that of Lancaster, but in those
rude times the age and character of the claimant were
important factors in determining the result of every
contest.

Henry IV, falsely deducing his title from Henry III,
was in fact an usurper, but his character and experience enabled him to sustain himself upon the throne
against the young earl of March, a child of seven
years, great grandson of Lionel, and the rightful heir.
The qualities of Henry's son, the famous Henry V, enabled him also to maintain himself upon the throne,
the very idol of the English people, and transmit the
crown without question to his infant son. The feebleness and incapacity of Henry VI, the third Lancastrian
king, obliged him to give way to Edward IV of the
house of York. *

Upon the death of Edward in 1483, the young prince,
his son, was at the mercy of his uncle Richard. Under
the title of Edward V, this pale shadow of a boy
king, lived but a few months after his father's death,
smothered in the Tower, with his brother, by order of
his uncle.

Richard   III,   the   last   of   the   Plantagenets,
then   usurped   the   crown,   but   his   method   of
acquiring   it   so   incensed   the   people   that   the

*For this period of English history, see Bulwer's "Last of the Barons."

Lancastrian faction again came to the front, and
rallying around Henry, earl of Richmond, defeated
Richard at the battle of Bosworth in 1485 and the
crown of England, worn by Richard in the battle, was
placed as the symbol of sovereignty upon the young
earl's head, and upon the battle field itself he was ac-
claimed as Henry VII, King of England, the first of the
so-called Tudor Kings. Shortly after coming to the
throne he married Elizabeth of York, the only surviv-
ing child of Edward IV, and by this marriage were
united the contending factions of York and Lancaster,
the White and the Red rose. England then settled
down to a state of comparative domestic tranquility
not to be again seriously disturbed by civil war for
over a hundred and fifty years.*

*For a proper understanding of the history of England from the de-
position of Richard II in 1399 to the accession of Henry VIII in 1509,
it is necessary to have a fairly accurate knowledge of the genealogy of
the different branches of the royal family from the time of Henry III
(died 1272, the sovereign from whom Henry IV claimed title to the
crown), to that of Henry VIII.

Vague and indefinite as these genealogical intricacies now generally
are in the minds of all but close students of that period, it must be
remembered that for more than a hundred years, with intervening lulls,
they were burning and vital questions, eagerly discussed in all their
details in the courts, camps and parliaments, as well as at the fire-
sides, of our English ancestors, and angry disputes were liable to be
followed, and in fact for a time (1455-1485) were followed, by civil war.
Some faint idea of the gravity and intensity of these disputes may be
realized by those in our own country who remember the excitement
caused by the Hayes-Tilden controversy over the Presidential election in
1876, when the Electoral Commission was appointed. Let us suppose
that commission to have been a failure, and to have been followed by
successive appeals to arms for about thirty continuous years, the theatre

The reign of Henry VII marks an epoch in English history, and is generally regarded as the dividing line between the feudal period and the foundation of the system on which modern society is based. In this reign the art of printing was brought to a state of comparative perfection, and improvements in the use of firearms revolutionized the methods of war, thus giving to civilization an easy victory over the barbarous tribes of the far off countries of the new world, then for the first time brought to the knowledge of Europe, and this discovery of America opened up also a new and ever-widening field for the energies of the adventurous English race. In fact, it was only by an accident that Columbus did not sail upon his first voyage under the English flag. His brother Bartholomew was on his way to England to engage the assistance of Henry in this enterprise, already brought to the king's attention, when he was taken and detained by pirates. Meantime Isabella of Spain furnished the necessary aid. Had Henry been the first in the field, what momentous consequences

---

of war being about the size of the state of Pennsylvania, the population being about three millions, with hostile neighbors on all sides, and we may have some idea of the Wars of the Roses. Let us then suppose the invention of some happy political device, whereby all the turmoil, confusion and bloodshed incident to civil war could be suddenly avoided, and we may be able to realize the passionate joy of the English people when Henry VII married Elizabeth of York, and the union was blessed with an heir, in whose veins was united the blood of York and Lancaster, and who was recognized by all parties as the unquestioned successor by hereditary right to the English throne.

would not have followed in the history **of our Western** world.

In character Henry VII was parsimonious, calculating, and suspicious. His dominating vice was avarice, and by means of many harassing and illegal exactions he became enormously rich, and at his death left to his son a private fortune estimated at nearly ten millions of dollars, an incredible sum for those days. Personally he was a very unamiable and unpopular sovereign, but did great service in settling and consolidating the kingdom which had been for so many years distracted by the "Wars of the Roses."

With the practical side of his character necessarily developed by the various and constantly present difficulties of his position, he was, nevertheless, something of a bookish man, a dreamer of dreams, and fond of literature and art. In architecture his memory will be always preserved by his beautiful chapel, the finest, perhaps in England, which he added during his life to the east end of Westminster Abbey.

In domestic affairs the appearance of two young impostors, Lambert Simnel and Perkin Warbeck, who, at different times, laid claim to the crown as being rightful heirs of the house of York, gave rise to insurrections which troubled, but at no time seriously threatened, Henry's occupation of the throne.

The enlargement of the jurisdiction of the so-called Star Chamber, a tribunal appointed by the crown and which now began to adjudge secretly **a variety** of ques-

ELISABETH OF YORK.
(1466-1502.)
Page 75.

tions involving personal liberty **and** property, **was** an
event of the greatest importance as increasing the
arbitrary power of the king. This iniquitous tribunal,
entirely at variance with the institutions of a free people, was ultimately swept out of existence by the Long
Parliament in 1641, though its hateful memory has
remained as a warning down to our own time.

In foreign affairs the policy and astuteness of the
king enabled him to make his influence powerfully felt
on the Continent without entailing any serious consequences in the way of expensive wars.

Of the Tudor sovereigns Henry VII is the only
direct ancestor of queen Victoria.

He died in 1509 at the age of fifty-two and was succeeded by his son Henry VIII.

The plaster cast here shown is in part a copy of his
full length effigy, in bronze, which lies recumbent upon
his tomb, by the side of that of his wife, in his own
chapel in Westminster Abbey. The sculptor was
Pietro Torregiano.

ELIZABETH OF YORK.

(1466-1502.)

Elizabeth of York was the daughter of Edward IV
and his queen, Elizabeth Woodville. When she had

reached the age of seventeen **her** father died, and her
uncle **Richard, by** the murder in the Tower of the young
princes, **her brothers, established** himself on the throne
under **the title of Richard III.** In order to strengthen
his title **Richard was** planning **to** marry his niece,
when, by the defeat at Bosworth, he lost not only the
crown, but **also** his life. Upon the accession of Henry
VII the people clamored for Henry's marriage with
Elizabeth, that all the turmoil and bloodshed of the
Wars of the Roses might cease with this alliance of the
houses of York and Lancaster. Henry, however, was
unwilling to have his own title appear to depend upon
that of his wife, and so postponed the marriage until
he felt himself entirely secure in his new position.
After his own independent coronation he married Elizabeth in 1586, and no marriage ever brought so **great**
satisfaction to a whole people as this. The queen was
an amiable woman, and always maintained a firm hold
on the affections of the people at large. She was devoted to the king, but he, on his part, was far from a
considerate husband. He hated the whole York family
and their adherents, and such troubles as arose during
his reign were largely due to his own unnecessary rigor
in dealing with the leaders of the defeated faction.

The full-length effigy of Elizabeth, in bronze, of which
this in part is a plaster copy, lies recumbent, by the
side of that of her husband, upon her tomb in the
chapel of Henry VII in Westminster Abbey.

The sculptor was Pietro Torregiano, the Florentine rival of Michael Angelo, and to whom the latter, in a boyish quarrel, was indebted for his broken nose.

HENRY VIII.

(1491-1547.)

Henry VIII came to the throne upon the death of his father, Henry VII, in 1509, at the age of eighteen, being the first king since Richard II, over a hundred years before, whose title was without a flaw.

In person he was handsome, athletic, and fond of outdoor sports, in which he excelled. Of an exceptionally bright and active mind he had taken kindly to the "new learning," as it was called, and was altogether one of the most accomplished men of his time. He was skilled in music, and even composed some pieces, and spoke French and Spanish fluently, with an excellent knowledge of Latin. In disposition he was bright and gay and full of life and spirit. His father, by a combination of extortion and avarice, had amassed a vast fortune of which Henry was sole heir, and the young king proceeded forthwith to spend his money freely, inaugurating and carrying out on a magnificent scale a variety of court entertainments, ably assisted therein

by his bosom friend **and companion, Thomas Wolsey**
Dean of Lincoln.*

For the first twenty years of his reign, Henry was one
of the most popular of English kings, and notwith-
standing the change that came over him, seems never
to have entirely lost the affection of his subjects. In
later life the impetuosity and ardor of his youth,
warped by the practically unrestrained exercise of
arbitrary power and the unrestricted pursuit of
pleasure, developed into a certain sullenness of temper,
arrogance, and cruelty that made of him a different
man. His matrimonial troubles are associated with
this period of his life and by them, in popular
estimation, he is best remembered. He was six
times married. His first wife was Catharine of
Aragon, daughter of Ferdinand and Isabella of Spain,
and mother of queen Mary. From her he was divorced,
after nearly twenty years of married life. The history
of this divorce, involving many complicated ecclesiastical questions, and resulting, with other causes, in the
schism of the English Church from the Church of Rome,
makes it the most celebrated divorce case on record.
His second wife was Anne Boleyn, an English lady of
private station, and mother of queen Elizabeth. For
her alleged, though unproved misconduct, she was beheaded. The third wife was Jane Seymour, mother of

---

*The career of Cardinal Wolsey is in itself so interesting, and the
period of his official life is so bound up with that of king Henry, that a
short account of him is included in this catalogue, though, at present, the
collection contains nothing recalling his personal appearance.—S. L. P.

HENRY VIII.
(1491-1547.)
Page 77.

Edward VI. She died peaceably, greatly regretted by
the king. The fourth was Anne of Cleves, a Flemish
princess, divorced shortly after her marriage, her crime
being general unattractiveness. A handsome pension
was allowed her and she continued to live quietly in
England, on excellent terms with everyone, the king
included.

The fifth was Catharine Howard, who, after
her marriage with the king, was proved to have been
such a very undesirable young person that the king
concluded to have her executed. The sixth, and last,
was Catharine Parr, a widow of mature age, who managed to ingratiate herself sufficiently with the king to
keep her head on her shoulders, and outlive her royal
husband.

Aside from these more or less personal complications,
there occurred many events which make the reign of
Henry VIII one of the most important periods in English history. The most far-reaching in its effect was
undoubtedly the entire separation of the English
Church from the Church of Rome, and the passage of
the "Act of Supremacy" whereby Henry, and all his
successors on the English throne, became titular head
of the English Church with no ecclesiastical authority
acknowledged outside the kingdom. During this reign
occurred also the suppression of all the monasteries
and the confiscation of their revenues by the crown.
Some of the richest and most powerful of the English

families of our own time date their importance from
this period, when grants were made to them of the
escheated property of the church. The rise and fall of
Cardinal Wolsey is also a dramatic event of the
greatest interest.

In domestic affairs, the Parliament was frequently
assembled, but, as a popular assembly, it had sunk to
its lowest level in the history of England, from the
point of view of political importance. It seemed content
to regard its duty as fulfilled when it had registered as
laws the edicts of the king.

The parliamentary system, practically inaugurated
under Henry VII, and continued in this and subsequent
reigns, entirely at variance with the spirit of freedom, must be held responsible for the excesses committed a hundred years later, which ended in the death
of Charles I upon the scaffold.

In foreign affairs, largely through the commanding
personality of Henry, combined with the European
complications resulting from the rivalry between Francis I of France, and the Emperor Charles V of Germany,
England played a more conspicuous part than at any
previous time in her history.

In the last years of his life Henry became enormously
stout, and being also in ill health, had to be wheeled
about in a chair, presenting a sad contrast both in appearance and in character to his younger days. He
died in 1547 in the fifty-sixth year of his age.

The original bronze bust, sculptor unknown, of which
this is a plaster copy, is in a private collection in
London.

Cardinal Wolsey.

(1471-1530.)

Thomas Wolsey was born at Ipswich in the year
1471. His father is popularly supposed to have been a
butcher, but on this point there is some doubt. Whatever his origin, he received an excellent education, and
at the age of fifteen took his degree at Magdalen College,
Oxford. He then studied for the priesthood and, as a
young man, held the position of tutor in the family of
an English nobleman. Entering the church, his extraordinary talents, backed by such influence as he had
acquired by his own merit, gained for him rapid pro-
motion. When Wolsey was first introduced to Henry,
about the year 1511, the future cardinal was about
forty years of age, in the very prime of life, a finished
man of the world, conscious of his own superiority to
the men around the king, and eager to obtain an opportunity for the display of his abilities.

The young king was about twenty years old, ardent
and impetuous, and delighted with his new position,
for an austere parent, up to the time of his death, had
kept the royal nose of his youthful offspring pretty
close to the scholastic grindstone. Being entirely
ignorant of the business of government, young Henry

had, therefore, almost of necessity, retained as his
advisers the men whom he had inherited, so to speak,
from his father, along with the crown, but who were in
no way adapted to enter into the gay life of the Court
as conducted under the new reign. In fact they were
aghast as they saw the lavish son engaged in dissipat-
ing the vast fortune of the avaricious father. Wolsey
at once took in the situation and saw that the easiest
way to gain the confidence of the king was to enter
with spirit into all the gaieties of the Court, while at
the same time keeping a close eye on the more serious
business of government.

In the intimacy incident to their common pursuit
of pleasure, Wolsey intimated to the king that he
could never hope to really govern so long as he kept
about him as advisers the politicians who had risen to
power during his father's reign. Henry took kindly
to the suggestion, and in a short time the clever church-
man found that he himself, as he had planned, was the
instrument selected to bring about the change. His
rise was rapid and within a year or two from his first
introduction to the king, Wolsey became practically
the real ruler of England, tactfully concealing, however, from his royal master the ascendency he had acquired. By skilful manipulation he managed to get
himself appointed to a variety of rich livings in the
church (his acquisitive faculty was strongly developed), and thus acquired a princely revenue, which
enabled him to indulge his inordinate ambition for

display. The passion for building also seized him, and
Hampton Court, the palace of Whitehall, in London,
and Christ's College at Oxford (originally called **Car**-
dinal's College), remain as monuments to his memory.
In the various diplomatic missions to the Continent,
required by Henry's foreign policy, the cardinal, as he
had now become, was generally selected as ambassador,
and his retinue on these occasions was more magnificent
than that of royalty itself. At home his train consisted of eight hundred servants and attendants, taken
from all ranks of society, for gentlemen, knights and
the younger sons of the nobility were eager to enter the
service of the all-powerful minister of state, who combined with his love of political power an ardent interest
in the art, literature, and science of his time. Wolsey's
career as a statesman lasted about fifteen years, and
his fall was the result of the withdrawal of the king's
favor, based upon the cardinal's lukewarmness at the
time Henry sought his divorce from Catharine of
Aragon. In 1530, the year of his death, he was arrested
for high treason, and was on his way to London
to be tried, when overtaken by his last illness.

He expired at Leicester Abbey and shortly before his
death expressed himself to the constable of the Tower,
in whose custody he was, in words so indicative of his
own character, as well as that of the king, that they are
here given in full: " I pray you," said he, " have me
heartily recommended unto his royal majesty, and be-
seech him, on my behalf, to call to his remembrance all

matters that have passed between us from the beginning, especially with regard to his business with the queen; and then will he know in his conscience, whether I have offended him. He is a prince of a most royal carriage, and hath a princely heart; and rather than he will miss or want any part of his will, he will endanger the one-half of his kingdom. I do assure you, that I have often kneeled before him, sometimes three hours together, to persuade him from his will and appetite; but could not prevail: had I but served God as diligently as I have served the King, he would not have given me over in my grey hairs. But this is the just reward that I must receive for my indulgent pains and study, not regarding my service to God, but only to my prince. Therefore, let me advise you, if you be one of the privy council, as by your wisdom you are fit, take care what you put into the king's head; for you can never put it out again.''

In character Wolsey was proud and ambitious. To his equals he was commanding and haughty, especially when any indication of contempt for his origin was displayed, and nature had so endowed him with the dominating spirit that, in his intercourse with men, the accident of their superior birth seemed but of trivial importance.

The envy and hatred of the members of the nobility were therefore the more embittered by the sense of their own social superiority, and his ultimate downfall was hailed by them as a great relief from the domination of

MARY STUART.
(1542 1587.)
Page 85.

a man whom they regarded as an upstart. In disposition he was lavish rather than generous. In manners he was persuasive and insinuating, when it suited his purpose, and, from the affability of his demeanor toward his dependents, was very popular with those who served him.

His intellectual capacity was of the highest order, as shown during his administration of the office of chancellor. On this point we have the testimony of one of his contemporaries, Sir Thomas More. With More as his authority, Hume says: "A strict administration of justice took place during his enjoyment of this high office; and no chancellor ever discovered greater impartiality in his decisions, deeper penetration of judgment, or more enlarged knowledge of law and equity."

Wolsey's death took place in the year 1530, in the sixtieth year of his age.

MARY STUART.

(1542-1587.)

Mary Stuart, Queen of Scots, was born in Linlithgow Castle, Scotland, in 1542. She was the daughter of James V of Scotland and Mary of Lorraine. Her grandfather, James IV of Scotland, had married Margaret, daughter of Henry VII of England, and she was, therefore, first cousin once removed to Elizabeth of England. Upon the death, without children, of queen

Mary of England, daughter of Henry VIII and
Catharine of Aragon, Mary Stuart was regarded by
herself and the Catholic party as rightful heir to the
English throne. This claim was the necessary result of
the refusal of the Catholics to recognize the legality of
the divorce of Henry VIII from Catharine of Aragon,
as being without the papal sanction. The legitimacy
of Elizabeth, Henry's daughter by Anne Boleyn, was
therefore denied by them, and hence arose the plots
and bitter controversies that finally resulted in the
death of Mary Stuart upon the scaffold. James V
died a few days after the birth of his daughter, and
Mary became queen of Scotland while still an infant.
At the age of six she was betrothed to the Dauphin
of France, afterward Francis II, and was sent to
the French court to be educated. Previous to
her departure for France her hand had been sought
for the young Edward, afterward Edward VI of
England, but it had been refused. In the year
1558, at the age of sixteen, Mary was married to
Francis, and for the next ten years her life was
an eventful one. In the same year with her marriage
occurred the death of queen Mary of England, and
forthwith Mary Stuart laid claim to the crown. Elizabeth, however, ascended the English throne with the
enthusiastic backing of her Protestant subjects, being a
large majority of the English people, and this indis-
creet claim of Mary was the principal cause of her subsequent troubles. Francis II died in 1560, and the fol-

lowing year, at the age of nineteen, Mary, with bitter
regret, sailed for Scotland to undertake the government
of her native land. The flame of the reformation had
burned fiercely in Scotland, and at that time the
country was practically under the control of the ministers of the reformed church, at least in matters of
opinion, headed by the fiery and eloquent John Knox,
and the position of the queen, throughout her life an
ardent Catholic, was made very uncomfortable. The
question of her marriage now became uppermost, and,
after much deliberation, Lord Darnley was selected, a
great grandson of Henry VII of England, and therefore Mary's second cousin. The marriage took place in
1565, and the following year a son was born, soon to
become James VI of Scotland, and later, upon the
death of Elizabeth, James I of England. Shortly
after the Darnley marriage occurred the affair with
Rizzio, Mary's clever Italian secretary, ending in the
murder of Rizzio in the apartments of the queen, at
Holyrood Palace, by Darnley and his accomplices. For
this act Mary never forgave her husband, and in 1567 occurred the murder of Darnley. Of this crime the earl of
Bothwell was accused, and in public opinion generally
adjudged as guilty. Whether or no Mary herself was
an accomplice was hotly disputed at the time, and the
controversy has continued down to our own time.
Three months after Darnley's death Mary married
Bothwell, who had divorced his wife for this purpose, and a cry of indignation arose in Scotland

which took the form of rebellion. The queen's forces
were defeated, and she herself, being taken prisoner,
was confined in Lochleven Castle, and compelled to
abdicate in favor of her infant son. After a year of
confinement she escaped from Lochleven, but the
forces she gathered about her were again defeated,
and three days later, to escape capture, she entered
England, May 16, 1568. Her object was to make a personal appeal to Elizabeth to assist a fellow sovereign in
distress, but Mary had made a miscalculation. Her
former claim to the English throne had made her a
dangerous rival, and for the next nineteen years she
lived in England the life of a captive. The active life
of Mary Stuart, during which she played the part of a
great historical figure in the personal and political
drama of her time, was, therefore, from 1558 to 1568,
between her seventeenth and twenty-seventh years.
During her captivity constant efforts were made to set
her free, the last and great conspiracy being that of
Babington in 1586. For her part in this she was tried
and condemned to death. In this conspiracy the vital
question turned upon the point of Mary's guilty knowledge of, and consent to, that part of the plot which included the assassination of queen Elizabeth as one of
the objects of the conspirators, and the placing of herself upon the English throne. Mary herself, while
admitting certain minor accusations, denied such guilty
knowledge, and in regard to this, as in the question of
her complicity with Darnley's murder, a bitter contro-

QUEEN ELISABETH.
(1533-1603.)
Page 89.

versy arose at the time and exists to the present day. She was beheaded at Fotheringay Castle on February 8, 1587, in the forty-sixth year of her age. She met her fate with resolution and dignity.

Mary Stuart was a woman of great accomplishments, both of mind and body. Beautiful in face and figure, she possessed, in a wonderful degree, the power of fascination. Beneath her charm of manner, however, lay an active and ambitious temper, and when carried away by her ardent loves and hates she seemed to stop at nothing to accomplish the fulfilment of her purpose. But with all her passion and her faults there ran throughout her character a certain loftiness of spirit which found its full expression when summoned to face death upon the scaffold, and during her life she never appeared to so great advantage as when called upon to leave it.

The original bronze bust, of which this is a plaster copy, is to be seen in the National Portrait Gallery in London, in the same hall that contains the royal effigies.

QUEEN ELIZABETH.

(1533-1603.)

Elizabeth of England was the daughter of Henry VIII and the ill-fated Anne Boleyn. She ascended the throne in the year 1558 at the age of twenty-five. A woman **of strong and determined** character, and called upon as an almost absolute sovereign to take an active part in the stirring times in which she lived, her name has become a memorable one in history. Fierce and bitter have **been** the contentions **that** have arisen in regard to her conduct in the various crises that arose during her long reign, and their echo is heard even down to our own day.

Foremost in point of dramatic interest was her quarrel, political and national, as well as personal, with her cousin Mary Stuart, Queen of Scots, culminating in the death upon the scaffold of her life-long rival. In extenuation, if not in vindication, of Elizabeth, it must always be remembered that Mary, representing political and religious ideas that the people of England regarded as dangerous to their liberties, throughout her life was almost compelled by circumstances to plot against the life and throne of Elizabeth. The last plot for which Mary suffered death occurred in 1586, and is known as Babington's conspiracy. The evidence, written and oral, was overwhelming, and Mary could offer nothing but her own denial, and a claim that the letters produced against her were forgeries. The English people, all too accustomed to the violent methods of the time, and remembering the cruel scenes enacted during the preceding reign of Mary Tudor, clamored for her death as their only relief against the continual menace of revolution, and the death warrant was signed by Elizabeth on February 1, 1587. An affecting letter written by Mary to Elizabeth after her condemnation, the scene upon the scaffold, and her sex, created at the time, and will always continue to create, profound sympathy for the fate of the Scottish queen.

The defeat of the Spanish Armada, fitted out by Philip II of Spain, to conquer England and to avenge the death of Mary Stuart, saved England from the disaster of even temporary Spanish rule, and was the principal event in the foreign relations of England during the reign of Elizabeth.

The voyages and discoveries of Sir Walter Raleigh are of especial interest to Americans. For the English-speaking race, the fact that Shakespeare flourished in this period makes the Elizabethan Age the most important epoch in the history of English literature.

The full-length effigy of Elizabeth, in marble, of which this, in plaster, is in part a copy, is a recumbent figure upon her tomb **in** the chapel of Henry VII in Westminster Abbey.

CATALOGUE OF PICTURES.

No. 1
p.95

Southampton, Long Island, August, 1912.

The following pictures, reproduced for this volume by the photogravure process, and numbered to correspond with the descriptions in the Catalogue, were obtained by me at the time and places stated in the text. Although the artists are for the most part unknown, the pictures, painted, with two or three exceptions, upon panel, are submitted as original examples of early Italian art. The sizes, given in inches, include the frames.

Among the objects of plastic art exhibited in the museum there are no examples of original work, the upward of seventy Greek, Italian, and English Renaissance reproductions being in marble, bronze, and plaster, those in marble, including the eighteen portrait busts of the Roman Emperors, numerically predominating.

Not included in the above enumeration are thirty-eight plaster slabs of the frieze of the Parthenon, obtained from the Metropolitan Museum of Art of New York. These reproductions have been placed under the cornice around the two main halls and in the smaller rooms.

With the exception of the "Winged Victory of Samothrace," which is smaller, and the imperial busts, which are larger, all the reproductions are of the same size as their respective originals.

S. L. P.

No 2
D 95

1

Madonna and Child.

Unknown Florentine. Fifteenth century. Painted on panel. At the bottom of the frame can be made out the Latin inscription: "Ave Maria Gratia Plena, D. O. M." Hail Mary full of grace, Deo Optimo Maximo (To God the best the greatest). Many decorative religious panels similar to this have survived in Italy to the present day.

Obtained in Florence in 1893.

47 x 22

2

From the Convento Delle Contesse, Near Foligno, Central Italy.

Evidently a votive offering, representing a young monk as donor of a church or convent with a di-

minutive kneeling nun. In Italian and Latin, on
the rim of the dais, are painted certain words and
numerals of which the following is a translation:
"Pray for Simone Lechovelia, MCCCCLXXI (1471)
Cosmere painted this." Painted on panel, frame
and picture being one piece.

Obtained in Florence in 1896.

59 x 38

3

Repose In Egypt.

Unknown Italian.   Sixteenth century.
Attributed to F. Baroccio (1528-1612.)
Obtained in London in 1881.

30 x 12

4

Madonna, Child and Adoring Angel Offering Flowers.

Unknown early Venetian.
First half of sixteenth century. Probably by some
pupil of Palma Vecchio (1480-1528).
Obtained in London in 1881.

30 x 26

5

The Virgin of Mercy.

Ansano di Pietro Mencio, called "Sano di
Pietro" (1406-1481). A painter of Siena, whose nu-

No. 3
p. 98

merous works are mostly to be seen in the gallery
of Siena, Italy. The predella belongs to an earlier
period. Obtained in Florence in 1896.

36 x 24

6

Madonna and Child.
Francesco Bissolo (1490–1530).
Pupil of Giovanni Bellini (1426–1516).
Bissolo's works are rarely seen outside of Venice.
Obtained in Venice in 1896.

49 x 37

7

Madonna and Child with St. John and Angels.
Unknown Italian.   Roman school.
Second half sixteenth century.
Obtained in Venice in 1896.

36 x 28

8

Madonna and Child.
Attributed to
Girolamo dai Libri (1472–1555). School of Verona.
Obtained in Venice in 1896.

40 x 30

9

The Mystic Marriage of St. Catharine.
Obtained at the sale of the pictures of the late
S. L. M. Barlow, in New York, in 1889. The cata-

logue at the time of the sale contained the following statement: "Giovanni Bellini (1426–1516).
This picture was taken from a gallery in Silesia by
the troops of Napoleon and afterward restored.
Purchased by the late owner upon the recommen-
dation of Sir Charles Eastlake."

36 x 27

10

Madonna in Adoration, with St. Joseph.
Unknown Early Florentine.

End of fifteenth century or beginning of sixteenth. Very similar in style, subject and color to
a picture in the Uffizi Gallery, at Florence, by
Lorenzo di Credi (1459–1537).

Obtained in Florence in 1891.
42 x 42

11

Madonna and Child. Unknown Early Venetian.
Byzantine style of fourteenth century.
Obtained in Venice in 1896.
52 x 37

12

Madonna and Child.

Unknown early Venetian. First half sixteenth
century.
Possibly by Boccaccio Boccacino or some unknown
pupil of Giorgione (1476–1511).

No. 4

Obtained in 1896 from the Palazzo Giustiniani
Vescovio, Grand Canal, Venice. Schiavone
Collection.
33 x 27

13

Madonna, Child, St. John and St. Joseph.

Attributed to Innocenzo da Imola (1494–1549).
A pupil of Raphael (1483–1520).
Obtained from the Palazzo Giustiniani Vescovio,
Venice, in 1896.
53 x 43

14 *twin (copy after)*

Madonna, Child, and St. Anne as Adoring Nun.

Unknown Italian. Lombard School.
Sixteenth Century.
Obtained from the Palazzo Giustiniani Vescovio,
Venice, in 1896.
34 x 28

15

Madonna and Child with the Scapular.

Unknown Italian.
Obtained from the Church of Santa Zaccheria,
Venice.
62 x 27

16

Madonna and Child.

Unknown early Venetian. Byzantine style of
fourteenth century.
Obtained in Venice in 1893.
26 x 22

17

Unknown early Italian. Probably early part of
fifteenth century.
Obtained in Venice in **1896**.
25 x 18

17 ½

Madonna and Child.

Unknown Italian. Latter part of sixteenth
century.
Obtained in London in **1881**.
41 x 35

18

St. John in the Wilderness.

Unknown early Venetian. Probably middle
of fifteenth century. Something in the style of
the Vivarini, Venetian painters of the island of
Murano, near Venice, where the glass works are
now situated.
Obtained from the Palazzo Pesaro, Grand Canal,
Venice, in 1896.
53 x 27

No 5
p 96

19 and 20

The Annunciation.

Unknown Venetian. Sixteenth century. In the second style of Bissolo (1490–1530?) as shown in one of his pictures, differing from the others, in the Royal Academy at Venice.

Obtained in Venice in 1893.

37 x 33

21

Portrait of a Woman.

Unknown Florentine.
End of sixteenth or beginning of seventeenth century.
In the style of Angelo Bronzino (1577–1621).
Obtained in New York.

30 x 24

22

Unknown Italian portrait of

Petrarch.

Obtained in London in 1881.

23 x 17

23

Flight into Egypt.

Unknown   Italian.   Style   of   Parmigianino
    (1504–1540).   Painted on copper.
Obtained from the Armenian monks in their mon-
    astery on the island of San Lazaro in the
    Lagoons, near Venice, in 1896.
14 x 13

24

Water Color Copy of Titian's Christ and the Disciples at Emmaus.

Original (large picture) in the Museum of the
Louvre. Of the seated figures, one represents the
Emperor Charles V of Germany, and the other
the Cardinal Ximenes of Spain. The youth in the
background is Philip II of Spain, and the figure
in workman's clothes is Titian himself.
    Obtained from a copyist in the Louvre.
24 x 19

25

St. Paul.

    Unknown. The picture is something in the
style of the Vivarini, early Venetian painters, but
the inscription on the top of the picture in some

No. 4
p. 98

Obtained in 1896 from the Palazzo Giustiniani
Vescovio, Grand Canal, Venice. Schiavone
Collection.
33 x 27

13

Madonna, Child, St. John and St. Joseph.

Attributed to Innocenzo da Imola (1494–1549).
A pupil of Raphael (1483–1520).
Obtained from the Palazzo Giustiniani Vescovio,
Venice, in 1896.
53 x 43

14

Madonna, Child, and St. Anne as Adoring Nun.

Unknown Italian. Lombard School.
Sixteenth Century.
Obtained from the Palazzo Giustiniani Vescovio,
Venice, in 1896.
34 x 28

15

Madonna and Child with the Scapular.

Unknown Italian.
Obtained from the Church of Santa Zaccheria,
Venice.
62 x 27

16

Madonna and Child.

Unknown early Venetian.   Byzantine style of
fourteenth century.
Obtained in Venice in 1893.
26 x 22

17

Unknown early Italian.   Probably **early** part of
fifteenth century.
Obtained in Venice in 1896.
25 x 18

17 ½

Madonna and Child.

Unknown Italian. Latter part of sixteenth
century.
Obtained in London in 1881.
41 x 35

18

St. John in the Wilderness.

Unknown early Venetian. Probably middle
of fifteenth century. Something in the style of
the Vivarini, Venetian painters of the island of
Murano, near Venice, where the glass works are
now situated.

Obtained from **the** Palazzo Pesaro, Grand Canal,
Venice, in 1896.
53 x 27

No 5
p 96

pl see opp p 160

19 and 20

The Annunciation.

Unknown Venetian. Sixteenth century. In the second style of Bissolo (1490–1530?) as shown in one of his pictures, differing from the others, in the Royal Academy at Venice.

Obtained in Venice in 1893.

37 x 33

21

Portrait of a Woman.

Unknown Florentine.
End of sixteenth or beginning of seventeenth century.
In the style of Angelo Bronzino (1577–1621).
Obtained in New York.
30 x 24

22

Unknown Italian portrait of

Petrarch.

Obtained in London in 1881.
23 x 17

23

Flight into Egypt.

Unknown   Italian.   Style   of   Parmigianino
(1504–1540).   Painted on copper.
Obtained from the Armenian monks in their monastery on the island of San Lazaro in the
Lagoons, near Venice, in 1896.

14 x 13

24

Water Color Copy of Titian's Christ and the Disciples at Emmaus.

Original (large picture) in the Museum of the
Louvre. Of the seated figures, one represents the
Emperor Charles V of Germany, and the other
the Cardinal Ximenes of Spain. The youth in the
background is Philip II of Spain, and the figure
in workman's clothes is Titian himself.

Obtained from a copyist in the Louvre.

24 x 19

25

St. Paul.

Unknown. The picture is something in the
style of the Vivarini, early Venetian painters, but
the inscription on the top of the picture in some

No 6
p 97

strange language would indicate a different origin.
Obtained from the Palazzo Pesaro, Grand Canal,
Venice, in 1896.
69 x 36

26

Madonna, Child and St. John.

Water color copy of Botticelli's Madonna of the
Louvre.
Obtained from Mr. Randall, an English artist,
while copying it in the Louvre.
36 x 27

27 and 28

Annunciation.

Frame and panel are one piece.
Obtained near Florence in 1891.
13 x 13

29

Arms of Pope Innocent XII.

A member of the Pignatelli family of Naples.
Pope from 1691 to 1700.
Painted on Wood.
Obtained in Florence in 1893.
60 x 40

30

Madonna and Child.

Unknown Venetian, in the transition style from the Byzantine to the early Italian. On the scroll in the hands of the child is written in corrupt Byzantine **Greek** an inscription **of** which the following is a translation: "Blessed are those who keep my ways."

Obtained **in Venice in** 1896.

46 x 37

31

Portrait of an Austrian Prince.

This picture bears date 1637 and is signed B. **Saarburg. Obtained from the Palazzo** Giustiniani **Vescovio, Grand Canal, Venice, in** 1896.

40 x 34

32

Madonna, Child, and St. John.   Unknown Italian.

Sixteenth century. Painted on canvas. Obtained from the Palazzo Giustiniani Vescovio in 1896.

Attributed to Bonifazio Veneziano.

47 x 42

33

Head of the Madonna.

Carlo Dolci. Florentine painter. 1616-1686. **Obtained from the** collection of the late S. L.

M. Barlow at the sale of his pictures in New York in 1889.

45 x 40

\ 34

Madonna, Child, St. Joseph and Adoring Saint.

Giovanni Buonconsiglio, called "Il Marescalco," a painter of Vicenza. Beginning of sixteenth century. The signature can be made out with the aid of a magnifying glass.

Obtained in Venice in 1893.

53 x 37

35

Unknown Venetian Portrait.

Sixteenth century. Obtained in Florence in 1896.

43 x 39

36

Enthroned Madonna, with Child and Angels.
Unknown Italian.

Latter part of the sixteenth century.

Obtained in Padua, Italy, in 1896, where it had been recently brought from the little town of Orestano, Sardinia, in a much damaged condition. Lower part restored in Venice in 1896. Painted on panel.

58 x 34

37

Madonna and Child.

Unknown early Venetian, probably end of **fourteenth century.**

Obtained from the Armenian monks in 1896 in their monastery near Venice, and by them attributed to Nicolo Semetecolo (1350-1400).

40 x 36

38

Madonna and Child.

Unknown early Italian.

Obtained in Venice in 1896 in a much damaged condition. Restored by puncturing the flaking **paint,** putting paste underneath, covering with **paper** and then ironing the paint fast to the panel **with a** hot iron.

37 x 27

39

Horace Walpole, Fourth Earl of Orford.

Artist unknown. Obtained in London in 1881.

33 x 29

40

Copy **of Rembrandt's** Portrait of Himself.

Original in **the Gallery of** The Hague, Holland, **and obtained in** that city.

33 x 28

No. 8

41

Landscape.

Attributed to "Old Crome."
Obtained in London in 1881.
23 x 19

42

Angels in Flight. Decorative Panel.

Unknown.

Obtained in Florence in 1896.
72 x 30

43

Copy of Giovanni Bellini's celebrated portrait of the

Venetian Doge, Leonardo Loredano.

Original in the National Gallery, London.
Obtained there from a copyist.
32 x 36

44

Marino Faliero, Doge of Venice, led out for execution
on the Giant Staircase of the
Doge's Palace.

Andrew Geddes.
Obtained in London in 1881.
22 x 18

45

Copy of Rembrandt's picture known as

"The Lady with the Pink."

The original is in the **Dresden Gallery.**
Obtained in Munich.
50 x 42

No. 10

No 13

No. 14

p. 99

No 18

No 20

p. 101

No 22

No 25
p 102

No. 31

p 104

No 32
p 104

No. 33
p. 104

No. 35
p. 105

No. 37
p. 106

REPRODUCTIONS IN MARBLE, BRONZE AND PLASTER OF ANTIQUE AND RENAISSANCE SCULPTURE.

GREEK SCULPTURE.

The history of sculpture among the Greeks represents a progressive development up to a point that has never since been equalled, followed by an inevitable decline, until in its latest period, the original creative faculty having disappeared, the sculptor was obliged to content himself with the reproduction, with variations, of already existing forms. These phases of development have been divided into four epochs.

First comes the archaic period, which includes the plastic productions which antedate the time of Phidias, when the Greek sculptors, more or less unconsciously, were still working within the shadow of the dull formalism of Egypt and the East. This period ends with the beginning of the fifth century B. C.

The second epoch, dominated by the vigorous originality of Phidias, represents the period of highest development, when the Greeks, in the full and assured
enjoyment of personal and intellectual freedom, following the defeat of the Persians, threw off all restraint,
and working with that certainty and precision, un-
trammeled by tradition, which is a condition of genius,
produced those masterpieces in architecture and sculpture which have been the admiration of successive generations down to our own time.

The third epoch was reckoned from about the time
of the death of Phidias and his immediate successors,
at the end of the fifth century, B. C., to that of the
death of Alexander the Great in the last quarter of the
fourth century B. C., a period of less than a hundred
years, when Scopas and Praxitiles and their immediate
predecessors, contemporaries, and successors executed
work of extraordinary finish and perfection, though
cast in a less heroic mould than that of the sculptors of
the older generation.

The fourth epoch, similar in many respects to the
third, dates from the conquests of Alexander to the
subjugation of Greece by Rome, 146 B. C., a period of
about one hundred and seventy-five years, when
the highest order of original creative force
had disappeared, though works of great power
and beauty continued to be executed.

And here it may be remarked that the ideal
creations of the artist are after all but the embodiment

of the aspirations of a whole people, so far as they can
be expressed within the limitations of art. No
great artist ever springs unheralded from the midst
of a rude and uncultured people. His inspiration must
come from his surroundings, which he in turn creates.

And so, as we look into the future, it may never be
that another community will ever hold within itself,
and be able to combine, the elements that made the
Greek supreme in the world of plastic art. With little
of the introspective spiritual life which is the out-
growth of the Christian ideal, the sensitive Greek mind
sought an outlet in the worship of the beautiful,
and regarding the body as the temple of a
soul that might be as mortal as itself, the
energies of the Greek were all bent in the direction of
creating forms of beauty, in the intellectual as well as
the material world, that would satisfy a longing that had
in it little of the spiritual aspiration as conceived in
a later age.

Reversing the fundamental doctrine of Christianity,
he therefore created his gods in his own image, and
with an artistic temperament that for some unexplained reason has never been equalled, the Zeus, the
Athena, the Apollo, the Venus, or the Hermes created
by him, each expressing some lofty attribute of mind
or beauty of person, or combination of both, stood for
eighteen centuries unrivalled in the world of art, until,
for a brief period, challenged by another school which
had also for its motive a fervent worship of the beauti-

ful, this time spiritualized by the element of religious
devotion. When Michael Angelo created the Virgin
supporting in her arms the dead Christ, and Raphael
painted his Sistine Madonna, the world **again** saw the
keenest artistic temperament, united **with the** highest
order of technical skill, develop an art which was sustained by a simple aspiration understood by all.

Then it was perceived that Phidias and Michael
Angelo, each the inspired interpreter of the sentiment
of the age in which he lived, reigned supreme in that
realm where the sceptre can be held only by him, who,
in his relations to the material world, approaches near-
est to his Creator.

How profoundly conscious the Greeks were of the
majesty of a great work of art is illustrated by the im-
pressive story told of Phidias as he stood before his
completed statue of the Olympian Zeus. He was then
an old man, and this was the crowning work of a long
life devoted to his art. As he gazed upon this re-
splendent statue, instinct with life, power, dignity and
beauty, he raised his hands in prayer, and implored the
living God to vouchsafe some sign, if the work were
pleasing to him. Then suddenly, through the opening
in the roof of the temple, there fell at his unharmed feet
a thunderbolt, and he knew that his work was accept-
able to the benignant father of gods and men.

Of the different epochs of Greek sculpture here exhibited at Southampton there is at present no example
of the archaic period.

CLAUDIUS.   NERO.   TIBERIUS.   GALBA.   OTHO.

VITELLIUS.   VESPASIAN.   TITUS   DOMITIAN   NERVA

Of the work of Phidias there are to be seen the copies of the more or less mutilated slabs of the Parthenon Frieze, and the reproduction of the antique copy of the head of Zeus. Examples of the third epoch are represented by the Faun of Praxitiles, the Winged Victory of Samothrace and probably the Psyche of Capua. Of the fourth period we have the Boy Extracting a Thorn, The Wrestlers, and The Laocoön.

In the above distribution of epochs it will be noted how closely they correspond to great political and social changes resulting from wars, defensive or offensive as the case may be.

To the four periods above mentioned should be added another, the Greco-Roman, when Greece, though conqueror, gave to the conquerors her literature and art in exchange for law, stability and order. Then it was, when the Republic was crumbling to pieces and the Empire being reared upon its ruins, that the hard-headed, practical Roman, master of the wealth of the world, entered the field as a connoisseur and collector. In the fierce rivalry that ensued for the possession of the treasures of Greek art, scenes were enacted that are but faintly suggested in our own day when collections of French pictures are exposed for sale in an American auction room. Victorious Roman generals, returning with the spoil of conquered provinces, brought with them as their most valued trophies the marbles, bronzes, and paintings that had adorned the temples and market places of Greece, and the palaces of the

rulers of those countries that had responded to Greek
influence, and the choicest specimens of art were set up
in Rome to be gazed at by the untutored multitude of
the imperial city, or hid away in the luxurious villas
of the Roman nobles. To what lengths of oppression
and extortion a Roman connoisseur was prepared to
go for the gratification of the passion of collecting can
be studied in the celebrated oration of Cicero against
Verres, pro-consul of Sicily, a province already for
many generations dominated by Greek influence, and
rich in artistic masterpieces. In the world of art "the
glory that was of Greece" was at that time transferred
to "the grandeur that was of Rome," and we to-day
inherit at Rome, Naples, Florence, London, Paris and
other continental cities, the magnificent debris of that
period of craze for collecting art treasures, the like of
which has never been equalled.

Though lacking in ideal original creations the Græco-
Roman period is rich in portrait busts, of which count-
less numbers survive, to be seen to-day scattered by the
hundred through the museums of Europe. The busts
of the Emperors here exhibited at Southampton are
examples of this period.

It is hoped that from time to time other reproductions may be added to this collection that will illustrate more fully the various phases of development of
the Greek as well as other periods of plastic art.

ATHENS AND THE PARTHENON.

The Frieze.

When the first great historic conflict between Asiatic and European civilization took place in the beginning of the fifth century before Christ, Athens took the lead in the defence of Europe. The overthrow of the Persian hordes of Darius and Xerxes at Marathon, (490 B. C.), Salamis, (480 B. C.) and Plataea, (479 B. C.) was the signal for such an awakening of the human mind as had never been known before. This extraordinary **mental** activity was, without doubt, stimulated, if not actually created, in the sensitive Greek mind, by **the** exaltation of spirit engendered by the devotion, **self-**sacrifice, and consciousness of physical courage, **called** forth and displayed in a successful defensive war against vast numerical odds, where liberty and civilization were at stake. Immediately following the Persian wars came the so-called "Age of Pericles," when the intellectual development of man reached its highest point. This was the period of culmination in the world of art, when the genius of the sculptor, the architect, and possibly the painter, produced a result that has been since unrivalled. A part only of the sculpture and architecture of the Periclean age has survived and, of all the creations in the latter field, the Parthenon, for beauty of proportion and design, by universal consent, is the one supreme structure of the world. To Pericles and Phidias is due the adornment

of Athens, whereby, in conjunction with the poets,
philosophers, orators, statesmen, historians, and cultivated men of every profession, native and foreign,
who sought her out, she became the artistic and
intellectual centre of the antique world, a kind of
magnificent open-air University town.* Thus it was
that, the traditions of learning remaining an active
force, she continued to exert, long after her political
importance had become but a memory, a powerful
influence, vibrating through the centuries down to
our own time. Pericles was the political leader of the
dominant Athenian democracy between about 460
and 430 B. C. United with his extraordinary capacity for political domination was a broad-minded interest in the permanent welfare of his native city,
that led him to exert every effort to make her the
wonder and delight, not only of his own age, but
that of many generations to come. It was his rare
good fortune to be surrounded by a body of men
who, for genius and ability in their respective profes-
sions, have never been equalled. For the purpose of
this account, however, we need select but three, Phidias,
Iktinos and Kallicrates. In the art world of Athens at
that time, Phidias, the greatest sculptor of all time,
was the master mind, and to him Pericles confided the
supervision of all the work connected with the adornment of the Acropolis. This eminence, originally a
fortress, as its name implies, rises from the Attic plain,

*See Note.

on which the city is built, about two hundred feet at
its highest point above the city of Athens. It is ir-
regular in shape and contains about six acres, almost
level, surrounded by a sustaining wall. Nearly in the
centre of this plateau, Iktinos and Kallicrates being
the architects, was built the Parthenon, dedicated to
Athena Parthenos (the virgin Athena), Goddess of
Wisdom, the tutelary deity of the Athenians. The
temple was begun probably 453 B. C., constructed
throughout of Pentelic marble, and finished in about
sixteen years. The marble platform, which forms the
base on which the structure stands, is 228 feet long
and 101 feet broad. The body of the temple itself,
called the cella, is surrounded on all sides by Doric
columns, forty-six in number, with an average height
of about 34 feet. In diameter these columns are a little over six feet at the base, and a little less than
five at the top. The cella is 194 feet long and about
69 feet wide. Within this sanctuary was placed
the celebrated statue of Athena, the crowning
work of Phidias himself. The interior of the statue
was of wood, on which was modelled, with some plastic
material, the form of the goddess, and this was then
covered, for the nude part, with ivory plates, while
plates of gold were used for the garments and
such accessories of adornment as were required. The
statue was full length, thirty-eight feet in height, the
head crowned with a richly sculptured golden helmet.
In the outstretched right hand of the goddess stood a

winged Victory, six feet high, holding a wreath, while
in her left hand was a spear. This imposing figure is
supposed to have remained in the temple, in all its ma-
jestic beauty, for about nine hundred years, when it fell
a victim to the fanaticism of the iconoclasts of the fifth
century of the Christian era, and from that time on no
trace of it has remained.

Of the plastic decorations of the exterior of the temple we have still the larger part of the so-called frieze
of the Parthenon, though in a more or less mutilated
form. The frieze encircled the exterior wall of the
cella. It was 524 feet long, 3 feet 3½ inches high, and
39 feet above the marble floor of the temple. Being
placed within the columns, just beneath the cornice of
the cella, the view of it was somewhat obscured by the
columns. On the west front, the frieze is still in place,
though most of that which has survived is to be found
in the British Museum, having been brought to England by Lord Elgin in the beginning of this century.
There are, however, twenty-two slabs still retained in
the small museum at Athens, on the Acropolis itself.
The plaster copies of about 147 feet of the frieze,
here shown at Southampton just beneath the cornice
of the main hall, are an exact reproduction, of the
size of the original, of a part of the slabs now
in London, having been made in New York from
moulds in the possession of the Metropolitan Museum
of Art. The subject of the frieze is a festive proces-
sion in honor of the goddess Athena. It is the work

of Phidias, or done under his immediate supervision, some of it doubtless from his own hand, and all of it breathing the spirit of his genius. Much of it was shattered or entirely destroyed at the time of the great explosion in 1687. At that time the Turks were in possession of Athens and, being hard pressed by the Venetians, made a last stand on the Acropolis itself. Their powder being stored in the Parthenon, a Venetian bomb set fire to the magazine, and this magnificent temple, till that time practically intact for over two thousand years, was blown out in the middle, on both sides, and so it has remained down to our own time. When seen from the plain below, in approaching it from either end, it still retains, though despoiled of its decorative sculptures, much of its ancient beauty. Only when one views it from an angle which permits the sides to be seen is the story of its partial destruction fully revealed.

Its history as a religious edifice is interesting. In the fifth century of our era it became a Christian church, dedicated to the Virgin. A thousand years later it was turned into a Mohammedan mosque, and a minaret was then added to it. To-day all unsightly additions have been removed, and it is preserved and shown as an almost sacred relic of antiquity.

A fine miniature reproduction of the Parthenon in its original finished state, with all its exterior plastic decorations, on the scale of one inch to twenty of the

structure itself, can be seen in the Metropolitan
Museum of Art of New York.

---

*Attica was a comparatively poor country, of very limited extent,
with but few of the many diversified material interests of modern
society. There were, moreover, but few religious questions, as understood in later times, to occupy men's minds, nor was scientific investi-
gation a prominent feature in the classic period. The result was, that,
being allured, to the same extent as in modern times, neither by the
pursuit of wealth, nor pre-occupied by scientific studies, or religious
controversies, the energies of as keen and subtle minds as the world
has ever known were directed to the study and cultivation of philosophy, literature and art. With what unrivalled results the Greeks
wrought, in these their chosen fields, is a matter of history. Hence,
enchanted with the intellectual luxury of philosophy, the simple doctrines of Christianity, as preached by St. Paul to the Athenians, were
"unto the Jews a stumbling block, and unto the Greeks foolishness."
Later on the acute Greek mind, joyously aided by the subtlest of lan-
guages, undertook the congenial task of weaving around primitive Christianity a web of metaphysical refinement, and Athens having given
way to Alexandria as the centre of intellectual culture, there arose the
different Christian, as well as pagan, sects whose bitter hatred and
sanguinary strife so disfigure the earlier centuries, when the streets of
Alexandria ran red with the blood of fierce and ignorant fanatics who
freely gave their lives in the attack and defense of metaphysical subtleties capable of being understood only by the acutest minds among
their leaders. For a brilliant exposition of the religious and intellectual condition of these times, see Kingsley's "Hypatia." Of the sur-
vivals of this period of turmoil, the most interesting are the Copts of
modern Egypt (the only descendants of the ancient Egyptians), and
the Armenians, neither of whom could ever be brought to acknowledge
the ultimate almost undivided sway of Rome, acquired by means of the
numerous œcumenical councils convened for the purpose of legislating
on the various questions of doctrine and discipline that arose in these
troubled times. Refusing to acknowledge the authority of these councils, both the Coptic and Armenian churches have maintained an un-
interrupted hierarchy from their foundation to the present day. The
Copts, now about 400,000 in number, claim St. Mark the Evangelist as
their first Patriarch. Though the well-known inherited tenacity of
character and purpose of the ancient Egyptians is strikingly exempli-
fied in the modern Copt, it is a curious fact that the American Presby-
terian Board of Foreign Missions has, within the past few years, gained

many adherents among them to modern Protestantism, principally through the introduction of excellent schools. To see our New England school masters, spare in form, intelligent in mind, and alert in manner, teaching the dark skinned little descendants of the subjects of the Pharaohs, interspersed with the Mohammedan boys and girls of the Arab race, in the very strongholds of the early Christian anchorites on the upper Nile, is in itself a most interesting experience for the American traveller in that most fascinating of countries.

THE FAUN,

BY

PRAXITILES (4TH CENTURY, B. C).

The marble original of the plaster cast here shown is in the Museum of the Capitol at Rome, and was found in 1701 at Civita Lavinia, on the site of an old Roman villa. The underlying sentiment which inspired this statue was a favorite one among the Greeks, when the worship of beauty and nature, and a keen appreciation of the subtleties of relationship among all created things, supplied so much of what, in our day, is represented by the distinctly religious side of life. The original of this celebrated work, and which served for a model of its kind, was executed by Praxitiles, and is supposed to have been set up at Megara, near Athens. Many repetitions of it have survived to modern times, but the one here shown is considered the most perfect.

Hawthorne makes it the keynote of his romance of "The Marble Faun," and his description of the statue is here given in full as a fine example of a high order of appreciative criticism of a work of plastic art:

"But we must do more than merely refer to this exquisite work of art; it must be described, however inadequate may be the effort to express its magic peculiarity in words.

"The Faun is the marble image of a young man, leaning his right arm on the trunk or stump of a tree; one

THE FAUN.
By Praxiteles.
Page 124.

hand hangs carelessly by his side; in the other he holds
the fragment of a pipe, or some such sylvan instrument
of music. His only garment—a lion's skin, with the
claws upon his shoulder—falls half way down his back,
leaving the limbs and entire front of the figure nude.
The form, thus displayed, is marvellously graceful, but
has a fuller and more rounded outline, more flesh, and
less of heroic muscle than the old sculptors were wont
to assign to their types of masculine beauty. The
character of the face corresponds with the figure; it is
most agreeable in outline and feature, but rounded and
somewhat voluptuously developed, especially about the
throat and chin; the nose is almost straight, but very
slightly curves inward, thereby acquiring an indescrib-
able charm of geniality and humor. The mouth, with
its full yet delicate lips, seems so nearly to smile out-
right, that it calls forth a responsive smile. The whole
statue—unlike anything else that ever was wrought in
that severe material of marble—conveys the idea of an
amiable and sensual creature, easy, mirthful, apt for
jollity, yet not incapable of being touched by pathos.
It is impossible to gaze long at this stone image without
conceiving a kindly sentiment towards it, as if its substance were warm to the touch, and imbued with actual
life. It comes very close to some of our pleasantest
sympathies.

"Perhaps it is the very lack of moral severity, of
any high and heroic ingredient in the character of
the Faun, that makes it so delightful an object to the

human eye and to the frailty of the human heart. The
being here represented is endowed with no principle of
virtue, and would be incapable of comprehending such;
but he would be true and honest by dint of his simplicity. We should expect from him no sacrifice or effort
for an abstract cause; there is not an atom of martyr's
stuff in all that softened marble; but he has a capacity
for strong and warm attachment, and might act de-
votedly through its impulse, and even die for it at
need. It is possible, too, that the Faun might be educated through the medium of his emotions, so that the
coarser animal portion of his nature might eventually
be thrown into the background, though never utterly
expelled.

"The animal nature, indeed, is a most essential part
of the Faun's composition; for the characteristics of the
brute creation meet and combine with those of human-
ity in this strange yet true and natural conception of
antique poetry and art. Praxiteles has subtly diffused
throughout his work that mute mystery which so hope-
lessly perplexes us whenever we attempt to gain an intellectual or sympathetic knowledge of the lower orders
of creation. The riddle is indicated, however, only by
two definite signs; these are the two ears of the Faun,
which are leaf-shaped, terminating in little peaks, like
those of some species of animals. Though not so seen
in the marble, they are probably to be considered as
clothed, in fine, downy fur. In the coarser representa-

tions of this class of mythological creatures, there is another token of brute kindred,—a certain caudal appendage; which, if the Faun of Praxiteles must be supposed to possess it at all, is hidden by the lion's skin that forms his garment. The pointed and furry ears, therefore, are the sole indications of his wild, forest nature.

"Only a sculptor of the finest imagination, the most delicate taste, the sweetest feeling, and the rarest artistic skill—in a word, a sculptor and a poet too—could have first dreamed of a Faun in this guise, and then have succeeded in imprisoning the sportive and frisky thing in marble. Neither man nor animal, and yet no monster; but a being in whom both races meet on friendly ground! The idea grows coarse as we handle it, and hardens in our grasp. But, if the spectator broods long over the statue, he will be conscious of its spell; all the pleasantness of sylvan life, all the genial and happy characteristics of creatures that dwell in woods and fields, will seem to be mingled and kneaded into one substance, along with the kindred qualities in the human soul. Trees, grass, flowers, woodland, streamlets, cattle, deer, and unsophisticated man! The essence of all these was compressed long ago, and still exists within that discolored marble surface of the Faun of Praxiteles.

"And, after all, the idea may have been no dream, but rather a poet's reminiscence of a period when man's

affinity with nature was more strict, and his fellowship
with every living thing more intimate and dear."

———

Obtained from the "Atelier de Moulage" of the
Museum of the Louvre.

GROUP OF THE LAOCOÖN.
Page 129.

THE GROUP OF THE LAOCOÖN.

The original **of** this celebrated group, now in the
Vatican Museum, was discovered in 1506 in the ruins
of the Baths of Titus, at Rome. It is supposed to be
the joint work of certain Rhodian sculptors, who lived
in the third century B. C., though by some it is accred-
ited to some unknown hand of a later date. The subject is taken from one of the tragic incidents **of** the
Trojan war, as recounted by Virgil in the second book
of the "Æneid." In that book Æneas is telling to
Dido, queen of Carthage, the story of the fall of Troy.
He relates how the Greeks, after a ten years' siege, being
unable to take Troy by force, resort to the stratagem of
the wooden horse. The Trojans, being divided in sentiment as to the treatment of the horse, are urged by
Laocoön, priest of Apollo and son of Priam, king
of Troy, to destroy it as an uncanny thing. He says
he fears the Greeks even bringing gifts (*Timeo Danaos
et dona ferentes*) and goes so far as to drive his spear
into the side of the horse to emphasise his opinion. No
sooner has he done so than a scene is enacted the climax
of which is portrayed by the sculptor in the group
here shown. The story can best be told in the following translation from the Æneid, the hero of the epic being himself the narrator:

"**Here another scene and far more terrible is presented to our sight and disturbs our breasts, all un-**

aware. Laocoön, Neptune's ordained priest by lot, was
sacrificing a stately bullock at the altar, set apart for
that high service, when, lo, from Tenedos (I shudder at
the relation), two serpents with great eyes bear across the
sea, and with equal motion shoot forward to the shore;
whose breasts, erect amidst the waves, and crests drip-
ping with blood, tower above the flood; their other
parts sweep the sea behind, and their spacious backs
wind in rolling coils. The briny ocean, foaming, gives
forth a loud noise and now they reached the shore,
their glaring eyes suffused with fire and blood, while,
with quivering tongues, they licked their hissing
mouths. Half dead at the sight, we all fly different
ways. They with resolute motion advance toward Laocoön, and first both serpents, with close embraces, en-
twine themselves around the little bodies of his two
sons, and with their fangs mangle their wretched limbs.
Next they seize the priest himself, coming up with
weapons to their relief, and bind him fast in their
mighty folds; and now grasping him twice about the
middle, twice winding their scaly backs around his
neck, they overtop him by the head and lofty neck.
He strains at once with his hands to tear asunder their
knotted coils, while his fillets are stained with blood
and black poison; at the same time he raises hideous
shrieks to heaven; such bellowing as when a bull has
fled wounded from the altar eluding with his neck the
missing axe. Meanwhile the two serpents glide off to
the high temple and repair to the fane of stern Trito-

nia and are sheltered under the feet of the goddess and the orb of her buckler. Then, indeed, new terror diffuses itself through the quaking hearts of all, and they pronounce Laocoön to have deservedly suffered for his crime in having violated the sacred wood with his pointed weapon, and hurled his profane spear against its sides.''

The sequel to the story shows how the Trojans then dragged the horse within their walls in fancied triumph. That night the Greeks concealed within the horse, issued forth, and aided by their companions, who had secretly returned from Tenedos, captured the city, and the Trojan war was ended.

The discovery of this statue, almost perfect, at the time when the reverence for antiquity was practically at its height in Italy, created a great sensation. Michael Angelo was present when it was unearthed, and regarded it as a marvel of art. Just after the group had been discovered certain Venetian ambassadors visited Rome on political business, and upon their return home submitted to their government a general report on what they had seen. The following extract from this report taken from Symond's ''Renaissance in Italy,'' will be of interest:

''The Venetian envoys, however, received permission to visit this portion of the Vatican palace, and the single entrance was unlocked for them. After describing the beauty of the gardens, their cypresses and orangeries, the greenness of their lawns and the stately

order of their paved avenues, the writer of the report
arrives at the statues:

" 'In the midst of the garden are two very large men
of marble facing one another, twice the size of life,
who lie in the attitude of sleep. One of these is the
Tiber, the other the Nile, figures of vast antiquity;
and from beneath them issue two fair fountains. On
the first entrance into the garden, on the left hand, there
is a kind of little chapel let into the wall, where on a
pedestal of marble, stands the Apollo, famous throughout the world, a statue of incomparable beauty and
dignity, of life size and of finest marble [The so-called
Apollo Belvedere]. Somewhat farther on, in a similar
alcove, and raised on a like pedestal to the height of an
altar from the ground, opposite a well of most perfect
fashion, is the Laocoön, celebrated throughout the
world, a statue of the highest excellence, of size like a
natural man, with hairy beard, all naked. The sinews,
veins and proper muscles in each part are seen as well
as in a living body; breath alone is wanting. He is in
a posture between sitting and standing, with his two
sons, one on either hand, both, together with himself,
twined by the serpents, as Virgil says. And herein is
seen so great merit of the artist that better could not
be; the languishing and dying are manifest to sight,
and one of the boys on the right side is most tightly
clipped by the snake twice girdled round him; one of
the coils crossing his breast and squeezing his heart, so
that he is on the point of dying. The other boy on the

left side is also girdled round by another serpent.
While he seeks to drag the raging worm from his leg
with his little arm and cannot help himself at all, he
raises his face, all tearful, crying to his father, and
holding him with his other hand by the left arm. And
seeing his father more deadly struck than he is, the
double grief of this child is clear to view, the one for his
own coming death, the other for his father's helpless-
ness; and he so faints withal, that nothing remains for
him but to breathe his last. It is impossible that human art can arrive at producing so great and natural a
masterpiece. Every part is perfect except that Laocoön's right arm is wanting. He seems about forty
years of age, and resembles Messrs Girolamo Marcello
of S. Tommaso; the two boys look eight and nine respectively. Not far distant, and similarly placed, is a
very beautiful Venus of natural size, with a little
drapery on her shoulder, that covers a portion of her
waist; as very fair a figure as can be imagined by the
mind; but the excellence of the Laocoön makes one
forget this and the Apollo, who before was so famous."

The plaster cast here exhibited was made in Paris
from moulds in the possession of the Museum of the
Louvre.

HEAD OF ZEUS.

The original marble head of Zeus, of which this
is a plaster copy, was found in the baths of Otricoli, in
Italy and is now to be seen in the "Sala Rotonda" of
the Vatican Museum. It is supposed to be a faithful
antique copy on a reduced scale of the head of the most
celebrated statue of antiquity, executed by Phidias,
and placed in the temple of Zeus (Jupiter) at Olympia
in the Peloponnesus. Like the Athena in the Parthenon,
already described, this statue was of ivory and gold,
and represented the benignant father of gods and men
seated upon a richly sculptured throne, adorned with
precious stones, gold, ivory, and ebony. It was the
last great work of Phidias, and more than any other
creation of plastic art aroused among the ancients an
admiration amounting to reverence, of which we have a
record in the accounts which have come down to us. It
survived uninjured for nearly nine hundred years and
was destroyed by fire in the fifth century after Christ,
when the temple itself was also burned. At Olympia
the remains of the temple can still be seen.

For a most interesting detailed description of **this**
statue see Lübke's "History of Art."

HEAD OF ZEUS.
Page 134.

HEAD OF THE APOLLO BELVEDERE.
Page 135.

HEAD OF THE APOLLO BELVEDERE.

The original full length figure, in marble, this being a plaster copy of the head, was discovered in 1503 at Porto d'Anzio, Italy, the ancient Antium (a favorite resort of the earlier Roman Emperors) and was removed by Pope Julius II to the Vatican Museum, where it is now to be seen in the Hall of Apollo. The author and date of execution of this work are both matters of uncertainty though it is generally assigned to the fourth epoch of Greek development in sculpture, being, roughly speaking, the period between the death of Alexander the Great in 323 b. c. and the subjugation of Greece by Rome 146 b. c.

The generally accepted theory now is that the so-called Apollo Belvedere is itself a reproduction of some earlier work, similar in this respect to the Faun of Praxitiles. In any event it may be said that for life, vigor and spirited treatment of a noble subject it ranks as one of the great plastic creations of antiquity that has survived to the present day.

THE WRESTLERS.

The original, in marble, of this interesting group is
to be seen in the so-called Tribune, in the Uffizi Gallery at Florence. The Tribune is a round hall, lighted
from above through delicately toned glass and contains
many of the masterpieces of the gallery, both in painting and statuary, being one of the few rooms in any of
the European museums where this combination is to be
found. The paintings belong to the period of the
Italian Renaissance, while the statuary is exclusively
Greek. The latter encircle the hall and the pieces are
five in number as follows: Satyr playing on a Cymbal,
Group of the Wrestlers, Venus de Medici, The Knife
Grinder, and the Apollino. This grouping together of
the art of the painter and sculptor produces a fine effect, and considering the celebrity of the Tribune it
seems odd that this method of distributing the artistic
treasures of the museums has not been more generally
resorted to.

Various conjectures have been made in regard to "The
Wrestlers." It is, however, generally recognized as
being a work of about the fourth century B. C., and
by one authority has been attributed with some confidence to one of the sons of Praxitiles, and furthermore
to be the very group mentioned by Pliny with admiration in one of his well-known letters which has survived to the present day.

It has been much restored.

Obtained from the "Atelier de Moulage," of the
Museum of the Louvre."

THE WRESTLERS
Page 136.

BOY EXTRACTING A THORN.
Page 137.

PSYCHE OF CAPUA.
Page 137.

BOY EXTRACTING A THORN.

The bronze original of this little figure is one of the most pleasing of all the works of its kind, and is among the treasures of the Palazzo dei Conservatori on the Capitoline Hill at Rome. Though the exact date of its execution is unknown, it belongs to the period of later antique Greek art, probably about the 3d Century, B. C., and the youth has therefore doubtless been sitting at his self-appointed and never-fulfilled task of extracting a thorn from his foot for something over two thousand years.

PSYCHE OF CAPUA.

The original half length marble figure, of which this is a marble reproduction of the head, is to be seen in the Museum at Naples. It was found at Capua, a town situated between Rome and Naples, which in the earlier days of the Roman Republic almost rivalled Rome in size and importance.

The sculptor and date of execution of the Psyche of Capua are unknown, but the statue is recognized as one of the minor masterpieces of Greek art and is supposed to date from the 4th century, B. C., and therefore to belong to the time of Praxitiles. The story of Cupid and Psyche, the latter being typical of the human soul, is taken for the subject of one of the pleasing allegories of the later classic writers.

In the marble hall of the villa Carlotta, at Cadenabbia on Lake Como, is to be seen the celebrated modern group of "Cupid and Psyche," by Canova, the sculptor having taken the moment when they first meet. The villa Carlotta itself, with its well kept and extensive semi-tropical gardens, is one of the most beautiful of all the Italian villas, and contains the original of the well-known marble reliefs by Thorwaldsen, representing the Triumph of Alexander.

HERMES.

Hermes, the Mercury of the Roman mythology, was one of the twelve great gods of Greece and was the son of Zeus (Jupiter) and the nymph Maia. In many ways he came nearer to the everyday life of men than any of the gods, and there is something in his attributes so pleasing that he inspires a certain feeling of affection. He was the messenger, herald, and ambassador of the gods and the lightness, ease, and grace of his movements, combined with like qualities of mind, make him always an attractive figure in the Greek mythology.

When only a few hours old his youthful activity took the form of stealing the oxen of Apollo, but being immediately found out and about to be haled before his father for punishment, he gracefully restored them and presenting his brother at the same time with his newly-invented lyre, as a peace-offering, they became firm friends. But his inventive faculty did not stop with

HERMES
Praxiteles

THE WINGLESS VICTORY OF SAMOTHRACE

Page 232

the lyre (made on the spur of the moment by appropriating the shell of a passing tortoise when making off with his brother's oxen) for to Hermes we are also indebted for the alphabet, the science of astronomy and numbers, as well as weights and measures. He was also the patron saint of roads, and the sign posts scattered along the ancient highways were surmounted with his image. He presided also over the gymnasium, and travellers as well as athletes looked to him for protection. He was also the god of commerce and of barter and traffic, and in all dealings among the merchants his name was invoked. He was also the bringer of dreams, and that the lighter elements of his character might be steadied by more serious employment, to Hermes was assigned the duty of conducting the souls of the departed across the gloomy Styx.

He was, therefore, taken altogether, a very versatile god, and in one form or another was a favorite subject among the sculptors.

The marble bust, with the winged cap here shown, is a copy of one of the many antique representations that have come down to us.

WINGED VICTORY OF SAMOTHRACE.

Of all the archaeological discoveries of this generation, the Winged Victory of Samothrace, and the

Hermes of Praxitiles, are considered the most important in the world of art.

The island where this statue was found, and from which it takes its name, lies off the northwest coast of Asia Minor, and in ancient times was the site of a temple much resorted to from the mainland. Here it was that in 1863 the scattered fragments of the Victory were discovered, and three years later brought to Paris. About the same time, in the same locality, a coin was found bearing the stamp of a female figure, with flowing drapery, standing on the prow of a vessel blowing a trumpet. The coin was identified as having been struck in the year 306 B. C. in commemoration of a certain naval victory, recorded in history, and it was then recognized that the large and apparently valueless fragments of marble left behind on the site of the original discovery might well belong to the statue itself. It was not, however, till 1875, that all the fragments had been collected and transported to Paris and put together in the Museum of the Louvre, where this magnificent example of one of the best periods of Greek art now stands at the head of the staircase leading to the picture galleries. In the plaster cast here shown we have only a miniature reproduction of the figure itself. The original marble in the Louvre, including also the prow of the trireme on which the Victory stands, is about twice the size of life. The character of the work, combined with the evidence furnished by the coin above referred to, fixes the date

of the execution of the statue **as** of the end of the fourth
century B. C., and assigns **it** to the school of Skopas,
who shares with Praxitiles, **his** younger contemporary,
the honors **of** the third great period **of** Greek develop-
ment in the world of plastic art, ranging from the time
of the death of the immediate successors of Phidias to
the time of the death of Alexander the Great, a period
of about a hundred years. Comparing the Winged
Victory with the most important creations of the preceding age of Phidias, we can note the change that has
come over the ideals and aspirations of the sculptor.
The repose and dignity of the Athena of the Parthenon
and of the Olympian Zeus now give way to the life and
movement of the Victory **of** Skopas, or to the ease and
grace of the Faun of Praxitiles, for while the Greek
mind still retained extraordinary vigor and originality,
these sculptors, both following and leading in the
change of taste and manners that had overtaken **the**
Greeks, sought expression for their art in a less heroic
form than had characterized the Phidian age. For the
purpose of illustration, let the visitor look at the head
of the Olympian Zeus, shown here in this collection,
and create for himself, however imperfectly, an appro-
priate body for such a **head, and by a** like process
create a head for the Victory. Then let him mentally
compare the two completed statues, and he will at once
recognize the difference between the calm dignity of
the one and the graceful movement of the other, and
in that recognition **will** appreciate how this difference

in the conception and execution of a work of art is in itself typical of the change that had come over the whole community in other directions than those immediately related to art.

NARCISSUS OR "THE ECHO."

The bronze statuette, of which this is a copy of the same size as the original, is one of the most pleasing of all the works of its kind that has come down to us. It was discovered about forty years ago standing upon a **vat** in **a** soap boiler's establishment, at that time **unearthed** at Pompei, where, in the darkness **of the house,** covered **with the** ashes of Vesuvius, the **boy** had stood for eighteen centuries, then as now silently awaiting the responsive note to the echo which never came. Of its history we know nothing, but that such a work should have been found in such a place, even though only left there in the hurry of flight from the doomed city, indicates how widely diffused was the love of art among all classes of the people in ancient times.

The original is in the Museum of Naples.

NARCISSUS OR "THE ECHO."
Page 142.

ANCIENT HISTORICAL BUSTS.

MARCUS AURELIUS.   JULIUS CAESAR.   CALIGULA.

HOMER.
Page 145.

HOMER.

The date and place of his birth are uncertain, and even his individuality has been questioned, though according to the most trustworthy critics, without success.

He is supposed to have been born, of Greek parentage, in Smyrna, Asia Minor, or in the Greek island of Chios, and to have flourished about 900 B. C., thus being almost a contemporary of David and Solomon, though of a little later date. The original of this bust is in the British Museum, and was found in the ruins of Baiæ on the Bay of Naples, in the year 1780. It probably adorned the villa of some Roman citizen, as Baiæ was one of the most celebrated of the watering places of ancient Rome.*

It was a recognized fact in antiquity that there was no authentic portrait of Homer of any kind and the busts that have come down to us, unlike most of the marble portraits of the Greek and Roman periods, represent simply the sculptor's ideal. Homer was the greatest epic poet of antiquity and is still considered the greatest of all time. He is supposed to have been blind and to have wandered from place to place reciting his verses. He was the author of many poems but the "Iliad" and "Odyssey," with some fragments of other poems, are the only works of his that have come down to us.

"Seven Grecian cities claim great Homer dead
 Through which the living Homer begged his bread."

His poems have been frequently translated into English. Among others are the translations of Chapman (time of Elizabeth), Pope, Cowper, Gladstone and William Cullen Bryant.

PERICLES.

The original of this bust is in the British Museum. It is supposed to be a Greco-Roman copy of an original

---

*The glory of Baiæ has departed, a few ruins here and there alone marking the spot. Julius Cæsar, Pompey, Marius, Cicero, the Emperor Nero and many other celebrated men of the Roman Republic and Empire had country houses at Baiæ, and the ruins of some of these are still somewhat doubtfully pointed out. Its modern counterpart, though differing in many ways, is Sorrento, on the opposite side of the bay.

PERICLES.
Page 146.

Greek work of the fifth century, B. C., executed during
the life-time of Pericles. **It** was found in the ruins of
the villa of Cassius at Tivoli, near Rome, in 1781.

Pericles **was the** most distinguished **of Athenian**
statesmen. **The** exact date **of his birth is unknown,**
but he grew **up** in the midst of **the stirring times inci-**
dent to the **defeat** of the Persians **by the Greeks at
Salamis** (480 **B. c.) and was** probably **born even** before
the heroic battle of Marathon (490 B. c.). His death
occurred 429 **B. c. He was the leader of** the popular
party at Athens **and throughout his long** public career
successfully opposed **the** pretensions **of the** aristocratic
faction. Through his eloquence, his commanding char-
acter, his talents and his devotion to the interests of
his country he became the unquestioned leader of the
dominant democracy.

The "Age of Pericles" represents the most brilliant
period of intellectual and artistic development, both of
ancient **and** modern times, and **is** recognized, **so** far **as
it can be limited by exact** dates, as the period between
460 and 430 B. c. During the lifetime of Pericles flour-
ished Socrates, the philosopher, and Phidias, the sculptor, **architect and** painter, the Michael Angelo of antiquity. **Under** the general supervision of Phidias, the
Parthenon, which **is** still recognized **as the** most perfect
of architectural creations, was built and adorned, besides many other public buildings which made of Athens
the most beautiful city of the world. During the "Age
of Pericles," **or** immediately succeeding it, flourished

many other men of the greatest eminence in almost
every field of intellectual activity, many of whose
works have come down to us. Under the leadership of
Pericles Athens attained her highest point of glory in
both war and peace and became the leading state of
Greece.

The high helmet here shown in the bust was supposed to have been worn by Pericles to conceal an unusual length of head, a physical defect mentioned both
by Plutarch and the Athenian comic poets.

CAIUS OCTAVIUS,

after his adoption by his great uncle, Julius Cæsar,
known as

CAIUS JULIUS CÆSAR OCTAVIANUS,

and later when Emperor of Rome as

CÆSAR AUGUSTUS

B. C. 63 to A. D. 14.

The long reign of Cæsar Augustus, B. C. 31 to A. D.
14, represents the most brilliant period of the Roman
Empire. It was near the close of his reign that Christ
was born. Augustus therefore was the Emperor from
whom went forth the decree that "all the world should
be taxed" (St. Luke 2:1).

At the time of the assassination of Julius Cæsar (B.
c. 44) Octavius, being then nineteen years old and the
recognized heir of his great uncle Julius, was pursuing

LIFE SIZE REPRODUCTION IN MARBLE OF THE SO-CALLED "PRIMA PORTA
AUGUSTUS." THE ORIGINAL IS IN THE GALLERY OF THE VATICAN.
Page 148.

his studies and learning the art of war in Illyria, a Roman province to the north of Greece. Hurrying to Rome he found Mark Antony, then about forty years of age, in possession and determined to maintain himself. The young Augustus was then, as at all times during his eventful career, equal to the occasion, and drove Antony from Rome.

Then followed a reconciliation, when Octavius and Antony (with Lepidus), representing the Imperial party, combined against Brutus and Cassius who sought to maintain the Republic. The defeat of the latter at Philippi (B. c. 42) left the former masters of the civilized world which they proceeded to divide between them. Later quarrels developing, Octavius defeated Antony at the great sea fight of Actium (B. c. 31) and thus became sole ruler of the Roman world. Practically absorbing within himself by degrees the executive, legislative and judicial functions of the State, as well as those incident to his later office of High Priest, and backed by the army, of which he was commander in chief, he established on a permanent basis the system inaugurated by Julius Cæsar and (while retaining the old Republican forms and a certain personal simplicity of life) became the embodiment of the Imperial idea and has ever since remained so.*

---

*The closest modern counterpart of the Cæsars is the Czar of Russia. The possession of Constantinople by the Russians and the assumption of a practical protectorate by Russia over the Turkish dominions would closely assimilate Russia to the Eastern Roman Empire.

The Roman world, wearied with the turmoils and contentions of the preceding half century or more, accepted
the sway of Augustus without question, and seeing the
civilized world, for the first time in history, in a state
of profound peace and prosperity under a single ruler,
became convinced of the necessity of such a form of
government. So strong did this sentiment become that
even during his lifetime altars and temples were erected
in his name and divine honors were paid him. **The**
month of August was named after him at that **time and**
has retained its name ever since.

The "Augustan Age" was **the** most brilliant **period**
of Roman Literature. **The** poets Virgil, Horace, **and
Ovid, and the** historian Livy all lived and wrote at
Rome during this time, and were the close personal
friends of the Emperor and his great minister of State,
Macænas.

The two busts here shown are authentic portraits of
the period, **the** originals being still in Rome. The
smaller one represents Augustus at the age of fourteen,
and the earnest, thoughtful **look of the** boy is one of
the finest things in marble that has come down to us
from that period. The larger bust represents him after
he had become Emperor, and is taken from a full length
figure, the original of which is in the Vatican at Rome.

The story **of the** struggle of Augustus for supreme
power can be **studied** with great interest not only in the
histories of **the time but** also in Shakespeare's plays
"Julius Cæsar" **and "Antony and** Cleopatra."

TIBERIUS CAESAR.
(42 B.C.—37 A.D.)
THE ORIGINAL OF THIS MARBLE REPRODUCTION IS IN THE HALL OF AUGUSTUS IN
THE MUSEUM OF THE LOUVRE.
Page 151.

TIBERIUS CÆSAR.

(42 B. C.–37 A. D.)

Tiberius Cæsar, second Emperor of Rome and stepson of Cæsar Augustus, is one of the most interesting figures in history, and doubly so to us as the man who, at the time of Christ, ruled the destinies of the Roman Empire. The peaceful reign of Augustus had settled in the minds of men as an unquestionable fact that the Roman world could be safely governed by but one imperial will, and to Tiberius was confided the awful responsibility incident to the position of sole ruler of that vast consolidated net work of civilized and semi-civilized communities whose final appeal for justice must be to Cæsar alone. Of all the members of the imperial household he was the best equipped for the task. His training had been of the most thorough kind—from his youth up he had successfully commanded the armies of Rome, and been employed in the most responsible civil positions, and his conduct had justified his selection. When upon the death of Augustus, 14 A. D., he was called upon to assume the supreme direction of affairs he was fifty-six years of age. His mother was Livia, second wife of Augustus, a woman whose talents, ambition, intrigues and exalted station at one of the most conspicuous periods of history have made her name a familiar one in the annals of Rome. The real character of Tiberius has always been an enigma to historians, but of the high order of his intellectual

capacity there is no doubt. He set for himself the **task**
of consolidating the imperial system inherited from his
predecessor, and so far as the Empire at large was concerned, the verdict of history has set upon his administration the seal of success.   In his own household
occurred many scandalous and disgraceful events, and
the tyranny and cruelty displayed by him and his
ministers of state within the circle of their immediate
surroundings have left an ineffaceable stain upon his
memory. Tiberius was a silent, self-reliant man, and
with a certain intuitive grasp of a situation that,
penetrating all disguises, made him feared and hated
by so-called friends and enemies alike. Master himself
to an extraordinary degree of the art of dissimulation,
no one could ever tell what his real opinion might be,
except to know that what his interest dictated that he
would do. His cold, clear, calculating intellect dominated the fierce factions of his household, and he stands
the very embodiment of the imperial idea.

  When an old man his contempt for the servility of
public life and general disgust **with** his surroundings
led him to retire from the **world, and** he shut himself
up in the island of Capri, in the bay of Naples. Here
he built a palace, the ruins of which are still to be seen,
and it is curious how to this day the traditions of
Tiberius seem to hover like an uncanny spell over that
beautiful island. At Capri were passed the last eleven
years of his life, for him a period of brooding melancholy, for there it was, as Pliny says, that he became

TRAJAN.   HADRIAN.

"the gloomiest of mankind." It was during this sad period of his career that the stories of his many crimes, cruelties and debaucheries are told, which, in popular remembrance, most cling around his memory. To Suetonius we owe the revolting account of the last years of the Emperor. This author, (who was private secretary to the Emperor Hadrian) two or three generations after the death of Tiberius, wrote a history of the First Twelve Cæsars, but he belonged to the sensational rather than to the philosophic order of historians, and just how far his lurid tales are to be believed is very questionable. It seems impossible that Tiberius should have continued to rule the Empire, with the firm hand he is known to have exercised, from the seclusion of such debauchery as this historian describes.

Wasted with disease, the Emperor died in the year 37 A. D. In his last illness, showing some signs of recovery, he was smothered to death by Macro, his chief minister of state who had succeeded the still more infamous Sejanus, executed by an order of Tiberius issued from his retreat at Capri. Though the fall of Sejanus stirred far and wide the Roman world of the time, there was enacted almost simultaneously another scene in the far-off province of Judea of transcendent import to the human race. Doubtless unnoticed except as one of the many passing local events necessarily incident to the government of a vast empire, where provincial factions strove for

the mastery, occurred the crucifixion of Christ. That
Pontius Pilate considered it a subject of sufficient importance to transmit an account of it to his imperial
master at Capri is a matter for conjecture only.[*]

Tiberius left no descendants living at the time of his
death, and was succeeded by Caligula. By order of
Augustus he had unwillingly divorced his first wife
and married Julia, of infamous memory, daughter of
the Emperor and widow of Marcus Agrippa, the man
who built the Pantheon at Rome.

The bust of Tiberius here shown was made from an
antique marble bust still to be seen in the Hall of
Augustus in the Museum of the Louvre at Paris.

---

[*]During the first century of our era the Roman writers not un-
naturally regarded the Christians as only an additional sect among
the already factious and turbulent Jews. After the great fire which,
during the reign of Nero, almost entirely destroyed Rome, in the
year 64, a general belief prevailed that the Emperor himself had
been the author of the conflagration. To avert suspicion from himself, Nero, in looking around for a scapegoat, accused the Christians, and a generation later Tacitus, in his Annals, in relating the
history of the fire, gives the following very interesting account of
our religion as seen through the eyes of an eminent Roman historian who, though unprejudiced through malice, had not considered
the doctrines of Christianity as of sufficient importance to require
an examination. The opinions expressed by him in the following
extract may therefore be reasonably regarded as the currently accepted estimate of Christianity among the educated Romans of the
end of the first century: "Hence, to suppress the rumor, he
(Nero) falsely charged with the guilt, and punished with the most

ANTONINUS PIUS

exquisite tortures, the persons commonly called Christians, who were hated for their enormities. Christus, the founder of the sect, was put to death as a criminal by Pontius Pilate, procurator of Judea, in the reign of Tiberius; but the pernicious superstition, repressed for a time, broke out again, not only through Judea, where the mischief originated, but through the city of Rome also, whither all things horrible and disgraceful flow, from all quarters, as to a common receptacle, and where they are encouraged. Accordingly, first those were seized who confessed they were Christians; next, on their information, a vast multitude were convicted, not so much on the charge of burning the city, as of hating the human race. And in their deaths they were also made the subjects of sport, for they were covered with the hides of wild beasts, and worried to death by dogs, or nailed to crosses, or set fire to, and when day declined, burnt to serve for nocturnal lights. Nero offered his own gardens for that spectacle, and exhibited a Circensian game, indiscriminately mingling with the common people in the habit of a charioteer, or else standing in his chariot. Whence a feeling of compassion arose toward the sufferers, though guilty and deserving to be made examples of by capital punishment, because they seemed not to be cut off for the public good, but victims to the ferocity of one man."

Following the accepted chronology of his life, St. Paul was doubtless in Rome at the time of the fire and during the subsequent terrible events above recounted, and the exact date of his death being unknown, it has been reasonably conjectured that he fell a victim to this first persecution of the Christians. In the preceding reign of Claudius the Jews had been driven out of Rome as a disturbing element, and also the Christians, on the ground that there was no practical distinction between them, the difference being apparently first publicly recognized in the time of Nero, an unconscious tribute to the labors of St. Paul, the Apostle of the Gentiles.

It may here be incidently noted that at this very time the destruction of Jerusalem was impending. Rent by civil and

ANTINOUS.

Antinous, the page and favorite of the Roman
Emperor Hadrian (117-138 A. D.) was the constant
companion of the Emperor in his almost continuous
travels through the Empire. He was drowned in the
Nile 122 A. D. The extravagant grief of Hadrian upon
the death of Antinous found expression in the many
statues and bas-reliefs which he caused to be made of
his youthful friend. In Egypt and Greece even temples
were erected in his honor, and he was enrolled, by imperial decree, among the gods. The story of Antinous
illustrates the religious degradation of the Roman
world in the second century after Christ, then beginning
to be so powerfully influenced by the rapid spread of
Christianity.

"In all figures of Antinous the face has a rather
melancholy expression; the eyes are large, with fine
outlines; the profile is gently sloped downwards, and
the mouth and chin are especially beautiful."

The above quotation is from Winckelmann (1717-
1767), the first great modern historian of classic art.

The original of the marble bust here shown is in the
Capitol at Rome, and represents the Roman ideal of
youthful manly beauty.

religious factions, anarchy reigned in Judea and the Roman
general Titus, afterwards Emperor, laid seige to Jerusalem, and
after one of the most desperate defenses on record, captured the
city in the year 70 A. D. The Temple was at that time

ANTINOUS.
Page 156.

destroyed, and from this, and the immediately subsequent period, is dated the annihilation of the Jews as a separate nationality, and their dispersion throughout the world. With what extraordinary tenacity of character and purpose this marvellous race has survived the endless shock and change of time and circumstance is within the knowledge and experience of all.

COMMODUS.

COMMODUS.

RENAISSANCE SCULPTURE.

RENAISSANCE SCULPTURE.

In the fifteenth and sixteenth centuries there arose in Italy, more particularly in Tuscany, a group of sculptors who executed works of great tenderness and beauty.

Following the sentiment of the period their plastic productions were mostly in the field of religious art, largely represented by decorative sculptures executed for tombs and altars, and as adornments for the walls and doorways of the churches and cathedrals. The work was done in marble, bronze, and terra cotta, and practically all of it has survived to our own time.

It often happens that some of the most beautiful of these productions are to be found in more or less unfrequented localities, and their discovery by the curious traveller is one of the great charms of a tour through Italy.

Among the more interesting of these minor sculptors, whose art was almost entirely of a religious or monumental character, sometimes introducing the portrait of the deceased to surmount the tomb, were Mino da Fiesole, Antonio Rossellino, Benedetto da Maiano; and, working in terra cotta, Luca and Andrea della Robbia. Copies of the work of all the above sculptors are shown here at Southampton.

In addition to more important creations, Michael Angelo and Donatello have left examples of this style of composition, and a Madonna and Child by the former, and a little St. John by the latter, are here exhibited, the one in plaster and the other in a marble reproduction.

As pointed out in the preceding short article on Greek sculpture, the Renaissance period differs from the Greek in containing an element of spirituality impossible to the latter, owing to the difference in ideals essentially inherent in aspirations founded on motives so totally at variance one with the other.

That the Italian genius could compete with the Greek in its own field is shown, however, in those works of Michael Angelo which are outside the domain of religious art.

At present this collection contains no example of this later period of the development of the genius of the great Italian.

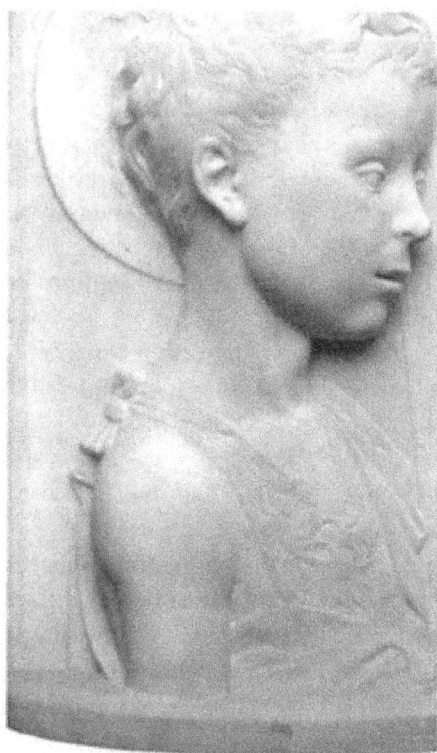

ST. JOHN.
DONATELLO.
Page 163.

MADONNA AND CHILD

Luca della Robbia

Page 163

DONATELLO.

(1386-1466.)

Donato Bardi, called Donatello, born at Florence in 1386, is generally recognized as second to Michael Angelo alone among the sculptors of the Renaissance. He has left many examples of his work, to be found mostly in the churches and museums of Italy. His St. George has been described as "the finest personification of a Christian hero ever wrought in marble."

The original bas-relief of the young St. John, of which this is a marble copy, is in dark stone, and is now to be seen in The Bargello (National Museum), at Florence.

LUCA DELLA ROBBIA.

(1400-1481.)

Of the numerous members of the della Robbia family who achieved distinction as sculptors, Luca was the eldest and best known. Though he executed work in marble and bronze, his fame rests chiefly upon his glazed terra-cotta work, wherein he confines himself almost entirely to the domain of religious art.

His original works are very numerous, and having been extensively reproduced, are widely distributed throughout Europe and America.

The original of the Madonna and Child here shown is probably to be seen in one of the churches of Florence.

ANDREA DELLA ROBBIA.

(1437-1528).

This sculptor continued for many years to execute the beautiful terra-cotta work which his uncle had made so famous, and developed a high order of creative faculty. He was assisted by his four sons, all of whom inherited in greater or less degree the talent of their father.

The Madonna, Child and Angels here shown is a copy in marble of one of the numerous productions of Andrea della Robbia, the original, it would seem, having been destroyed in the Cathedral of Messina at the time of the great earthquake, December 28, 1908.

ANTONIO ROSSELLINO.

(1427-1490).

Rossellino, who came of a family of sculptors, was born in Florence in 1427, and was a pupil of Donatello. He has left many works marked by delicacy of treatment and sweetness of expression, attributes in fact of all this group of sculptors.

The Madonna and Child here shown in marble is in part a copy of a sculptured memorial tablet to be seen in the church of Santa Croce, in Florence, on a pillar just opposite the tomb of Michael Angelo.

MINO DA FIESOLE.

(1432-1486).

Mino di Giovanni, called "da Fiesole," was born in the neighborhood of Florence in the year 1432. He executed many altar pieces and tombs of great beauty, and his bust of Bishop Salutati, to be seen in the church at Fiesole, surmounting the tomb of the Bishop, is one of the most striking portrait busts in existence. The original of the marble copy of the Madonna and Child here shown is in the Bargello at Florence.

BENEDETTO DA MAIANO.

(1442-1497.)

This sculptor, who shared with his brother Giuliano the fame of an architect as well as sculptor, was the son of a stonecutter and was born in Florence in 1442. He executed many works of great beauty, among others the celebrated pulpit in the church of Santa Croce, Florence, which has been described as "the most beautiful pulpit in Italy." Of his well known works there is also the shrine of San Bartolo in the Church of St. Agostino, in S. Gimignano, near Siena, and the Madonna and Child here shown is a copy of one of the details of that shrine.

MADONNA AND CHILD.

BY MICHAEL ANGELO.

The marble original of this group is in the Church **of** Notre Dame at Bruges, Belgium. Some doubt has arisen as to whether it be the work of Michael Angelo himself or one of his pupils. The better authorities believe it to be by the master himself, accounting for some technical faults on the ground that it was a youthful production, while other boldly proclaim it, in essentials, one of **the** sculptor's masterpieces.

MADONNA AND **CHILD.**

BY MICHAEL ANGELO.

The original is in the Bargello at Florence, and is one of the many more or less unfinished works of the sculptor.

LA FEMME INCONNUE.

SCULPTOR UNKNOWN.

The original of this well-known head is in the Museum of the Louvre, and belongs to the second half of the Fifteenth Century, Neapolitan School.

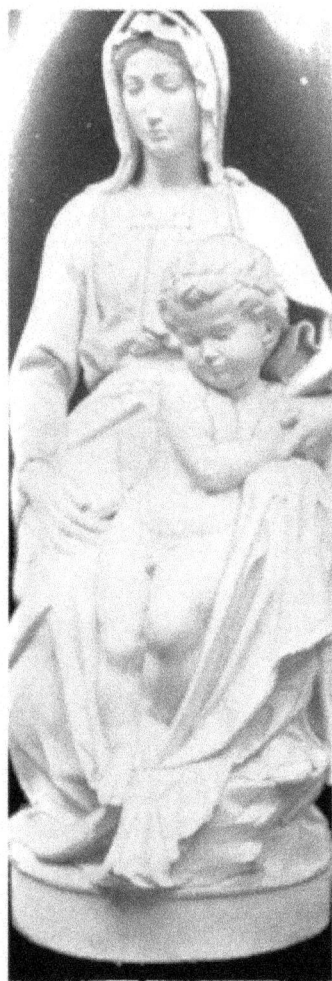

MADONNA AND CHILD

MICHAEL ANGELO

Page 208

Page 166.

LA BELLE INCONNUE
Florence

RENAISSANCE HISTORICAL BUSTS.

DANTE.
Page 167.

DANTE ALIGHIERI.

(1265-1321.)

Dante, "that singular splendour of the Italian race," as Boccaccio calls him, stands out as one of the great figures of history in the intellectual world. In the fourteenth and beginning of the fifteenth centuries Italy stood upon the threshold of that wonderful awakening of the mind which was to regenerate mankind, and bring back into the world some of that old time spirit of free inquiry and independence of thought that was to bear such fruit in the progressive development of modern civilization. Of this period Dante was the great precursor.

He was born in Florence in 1265, and from his own writings we learn of his aspirations and strivings from his childhood to the end of his career. At the age of nine he first met the little Beatrice, a year younger than himself, and from this time on, as child and woman, her image, whether present or only as a memory, becomes the inspiration of his intellectual and spiritual life.

Though poet, scholar and philosopher, he was an active participant in all the turmoil and confusion of his time, when the true principles of liberty were ever sought and never found amidst the faction and bloodshed of that disordered period. It was this disappointed dream of Italian unity and liberty, coincident with respect for law and authority, in both the civil

and religious world, **only** partially realized within our **own time, that** makes **of** Dante such a pathetic figure **in his longings for** the unattainable, when Pope and **Emperor, Guelph** and Ghibelline, struggled for the mastery, now **one and then** the other in the ascendant. During his maturer years **the poet cast in** his lot with the Ghibelline faction, **and at about the** age of thirty-six found himself **an exiled fugitive** from his native city, destined never **to return.** For twenty years he was **a** wanderer **seeking such** shelter as he might obtain **at** the courts of **the** petty Italian princes, but ever **anxiously** awaiting a change of fortune that would en-**able** him to return to his beloved Florence, the one great hope of his life. It was during this weary period, broken in fortune but not in spirit, that he composed his Comedia, as he called it. In the Inferno, Purgatorio, and Paradiso we have a vivid panorama not only of the age in which he lived, but of by-gone times as well, **his** keen insight penetrating the characters and motives **of the** great historical figures of the past as well as **of the** men and women he had known on earth, and whose tortures in hell for their many crimes, or bliss in Heaven, he describes. Throughout **the** poem, written in Italian, till then but the rude language of the people, there runs an elevation of thought and style that well earned for it the title of divine, given in the following generation by common consent, when the full purport of what the poet had written began **to** be understood. Then it was that, the matter

being of universal application **and** worthy **of the form,**
Dante was recognized, with ever-increasing appreciation
of his genius, as one of the great teachers of mankind,
and for six hundred years the translator and annotator
have been busy with his work. Fifty years after his
death there was established **at** Florence a public lecture-
ship for the elucidation of **the** Divine Comedy, with
Boccaccio as the first incumbent of what might be called
this chair of philosophy, history, science, theology, and
classical literature combined, for Dante was master of
all the learning of his **time,** and throughout his **poem**
there runs in rich imagery his philosophic thought
upon all these subjects.

In person he was spare in form and of middle height,
somewhat stooping, of a dignified and retiring manner,
with a sad, strong, thoughtful face. Studious of habit he
was usually a silent man, given much to solitude and
communing with his own thoughts, though capable on
occasion of fiery eloquence. Described by one of his
contemporaries he appears as "this Dante on account of
his learning was a little haughty, and shy, and dis-
dainful and like a philosopher, almost ungracious, he
knew not how to deal with unlettered folk."

Of music and painting he was very fond, and was on
terms of intimate friendship with Giotto, who has left
us the poet's portrait still to be seen on the walls of
the little chapel in the Bargello at Florence.

Dante died in 1321 in the fifty-seventh year of his age,
at Ravenna, where he now lies buried. In Florence in

recent years, a great monument has been erected to his memory in the square which fronts the Church of Santa Croce.

The original of the marble bust here shown is supposed to have been made from a death mask and gives the quality of his face, as described by Boccaccio, with greater apparent fidelity than the portrait by Giotto, which was taken in his younger years before the lines of his face were so deeply **drawn** by thought and mental suffering.

MICHÆL ANGELO BUONARROTI.

1475-1563.

The name of Michæl Angelo stands pre-eminent in the world of art, for it was he who, more than any other single individual, embodied the spirit of that awakening of the human mind after a sleep of a thousand years, known as the Renaissance.

Sculptor, painter, architect and poet, he excelled in everything he undertook, and has left for the admiration of successive generations the most enduring monuments of his genius. In painting we have his ceiling in the Sistine Chapel at Rome, adorned with frescoes representing the Creation and other scenes from the Old Testament, conceived and executed with a dignity and power unrivalled in the history of art. In

MICHAEL ANGELO
Page 170

sculpture we have his innumerable monuments scattered throughout the churches and museums of Europe, though mostly to be found in Italy, especially at Florence and Rome. In architecture he has left us the dome of St. Peters at Rome, and in literature his sonnets. As a military engineer we have the memory of his defence of Florence at the time he undertook the construction of the fortifications of his adopted city. He died in Rome in the year 1563 at almost ninety years of age, and lies buried in Florence.

His life, though crowned with so great achievement, had been full of struggle, and sorrow, and disappointment. His lofty genius, combined with the vehemence and intensity of his nature (the terribilità of his Italian biographers), had tended to isolate him from the companionship of men. From his youth an ardent student and hard worker, he was nearly always dissatisfied with his work, and left many things unfinished.

"In disposition he was proud and passionate, but high minded, not greedy of gold, but princely in his generosity. His mind was full of great conceptions."

———

The original bust, made by one of his pupils, of which this is a copy, surmounts his tomb in the church of Santa Croce, the Westminster Abbey of Florence.

MILTON.

1608–1672.

John Milton was born in London in the year 1608, during the early part of the reign of James I of England. At the age of sixteen he entered Christ's College, Cambridge, and going through the regular collegiate course of study took the usual academic degrees. It appears that during his university life, though his literary pre-eminence was admitted by all, he was unpopular among the students, owing to his self-assertion and conceit. He himself admits "a certain niceness of nature, an honest haughtiness and self-esteem of what I was or what I might be." At the age of twenty-four, after his graduation, he was in some doubt as to his career, meditating either the Church or the Law as his future profession. With the consent of his father, a London scrivener, he devoted his time to leisure and study, and lived pleasantly in the country near Windsor, about seventeen miles from London, where he wrote many of his minor poems, including L'Allegro and Il Penseroso, and later Comus and Lycidas, with Latin letters and Greek translations. At the age of thirty he traveled for a year or more on the Continent and especially in Italy. The memory of that period always remained one of the great pleasures of his life. Devotion to study had affected his eyesight and in 1654, at the age of forty-six, he became totally blind. In 1667 was published the great poem by which he is best known "Paradise Lost," on which he had meditated deeply for many years.

MILTON.

Page 172.

Milton, though one of the greatest of English poets, was personally a stern, unlovable man and unhappy in his **domestic** life. **Much** of his time **was** devoted to fierce political controversy during the exciting times in which he lived, which covered the downfall and execution of Charles I, the rise of Oliver Cromwell, and the Restoration.

In sustained **stateliness** and grandeur of style he stands **unrivalled among the** poets of the English-speaking race.

———

The original of the marble bust here shown is in **London.**

Southampton, Long Island, N. Y.,

August, 1912.

The following pictures, reproduced for this volume by the photogravure process, have been contributed to the Museum by Mr. James C. Parrish.

The two copies, after Raphael and Leonardo da Vinci respectively, were painted by Mr. Z. Alexandre of Paris. The original of the **Joanna of** Aragon now hangs in the long room of the **Gallery of The** Louvre. The "Mona Lisa," which was **hung in the** Salon Carré, was stolen from The Louvre **in 1911,** and had not been recovered at the time this Catalogue was issued.

S. L. P.

No 1

M. F. Harmsele

No. 4

after Leonardo da Vinci

1

Wife of Burgomaster Van der Horst.

M. J. Mierevelt.
(1567-1641)
54 x 43

2

Portrait of a Dutch Lady.

Jacob Van Oost, Jr.
(1639-1713).
41 x 35

3

Jeanne d'Aragon.

After Raphael
58 x 48

4

Mona Lisa.

After Leonardo da Vinci.
42 x 32

INDEX.

INDEX.

www.ingramcontent.com/pod-product-compliance
Lightning Source LLC
Chambersburg PA
CBHW031401270326
41929CB00010BA/1279